TELEPHONE

essays in two voices

Telephone

FIRST EDITION

Printed in the United States of America
ISBN 978-1-7348167-3-0

DESIGN ≈ SEVY PEREZ
Text in Sofia Pro, Proforma, and Adobe Caslon Pro

This book is published by the

Cleveland State University Poetry Center
csupoetrycenter.com
2121 Euclid Avenue, Cleveland, Ohio 44115-2214

and is distributed by

SPD / Small Press Distribution, Inc.
spdbooks.org
1341 Seventh Street Berkeley, California 94710-1409

A CATALOG RECORD FOR THIS TITLE IS
AVAILABLE FROM THE LIBRARY OF CONGRESS

TELEPHONE

essays in two voices

Brenda Miller

and

Julie Marie Wade

Dedicated to all our loves

This book collects a series of essays written collaboratively by the two authors over a span of four years. In this shared process, the inciting word (usually the title) spurs associative images from our personal and cultural histories. We build our pieces by responding to each other's writing until a natural endpoint occurs. Our interactions build a relationship, too, with each gesture requiring trust and vulnerability—not only to each other, but to the writing itself. We have chosen not to label the speaker in each section so that our individual voices surrender into a more collective, and communal, authorship.

Telephone

In the beginning was the gray, and it was called Elisha. In the beginning was the bell, and it was called Alexander. In the beginning was an office in Highland Park, a classroom in Boston, competing laboratories. One future hinged on the "harmonic telegraph"—better than a letter, better than a message in a bottle. Think of it: *your own words in real time, your own voice coming through the line like music, and there on the end, your beloved rapt and eager, listening, waiting to hear!* In this beginning, as with all: a diagram, a caveat, a rival creation story.

Imagine the bell chiming in the gray. Imagine the loud moon of sound rising through the clouds. Now Alexander whispers to Elisha on the courthouse stairs, "We can't all be famous, Man." In this version, he has a pipe and pretty hair, soft like taffeta on a woman's dressing gown. "Give it a century or so. History might turn this all around."

"Since when?" Elisha spits. He tugs his beard to a narrow point, then tucks his hands inside his trouser pockets. "Since when has history ever been kind to the underdog?"

When the red curtains sweep closed, the gold tassels swish this way and that, almost an echo. Over the clatter of applause, everyone hears it—that loud moon of sound, so unmistakable now: a bright silver telephone ringing.

•—•

Can you hear it? The song of a loon—voice echoing across a bright sliver of lake, disembodied. Like the voice on the other end of the telephone. In the beginning, that voice mingled with static, especially long distance, and long distance was expensive. My mother hissed the words to us as she spoke with her mother in Brooklyn—*long distance*—when we made a racket in the kitchen. She stood at the tall counter as she talked, the long coil of the telephone looped around her fingers. Her fingers twirled the loops tighter until her knuckles bulged, and then she let the strand uncoil, bouncing ringlets, like the hair of the girls I admired in novels.

I tried to imagine it: *long distance*, and how a voice could traverse that territory to reach us there in the suburbs of Los Angeles. My mother's voice, as she talked, became increasingly inflected with New York-ese, an actual dialect recorded by linguists; she seemed to take on the persona of a different person, the girl I never knew.

When my cousins came to visit, they spoke a foreign language, tough and hardy, a rollick through the streets. They said I had an accent too—a California twang—but I couldn't catch it. Can we ever hear ourselves clearly? How others hear us? *Say hello to your grandmother*, my mother said, and handed the earpiece to me. *Hello?* I said into the static, my greeting always a question, each word that followed echoing across the distance between us. The telephone warm with my mother's ear, her fervent listening.

•—•

My father's palm warms the receiver with sweat. His dime slides down the phone's cool throat. As he waits for a dial tone, he peers through the grate on the hospital window. It's late evening, September in Seattle, plump pigeons mingling on the ledge. He's calling his wife's mother, a woman they haven't seen or spoken to in years. His voice wavers when she answers, but then he says it, clear as a bell, "You're a grandmother!" Silence: looping back on itself like a snake's tail. "Did you hear what

I said, Tena?" She sighs, begins to uncoil. When she speaks at last, her tone is merely curious: "Boy or girl?" This is the first time my father has ever mentioned me aloud, and she can hear the hope and love and fear passing through his teeth like water over rocks. Love is an actual dialect recorded by linguists, as is disappointment, as is grief. "We have a daughter," he tells her proudly. The pigeons have moved on to other perches. A lone taxi glides through the street like a pat of butter. My grandmother lays the phone back in its cradle.

•—•

We listen for it, know by heart this dialect: a phone ringing in the middle of the night. A phone ringing at 9 AM, 1 PM, 6 PM, even 9 PM: these calls have an aura of polite questioning (*who's calling please?*). These calls are interrogatives. But a phone ringing at 4 AM: these calls use the syntax of the imperative (*who's calling!*).

Jerked from the warm confines of sleep, my mother fumbled for her glasses (*I can't hear without my glasses on*). In our bedrooms, we heard the phone jangling, water over rocks gaining in volume, the roar of rapids approaching. And then murmured words, *oh no*—water easing out into ripples against the shore. We huddled in our parents' doorway, the light from the bedside lamp wan in the wee hours. The phone, cradled, stubborn and silent, while my mother wept in my father's arms. They sat upright against the headboard, in their pajamas, covers still demure against their legs. *Go back to bed.* This moment: not meant for us to witness.

So we went back to our beds, in rooms that held no phones, not yet. Our rooms contained only the present, could not be intruded upon via *long distance*. Our rooms connected to no other place or time—sported no cables or wires, inlets or outlets. The air: undisturbed but for our own errant interrogatives, imperatives. We wondered what words murmured through the telephone line at that hour: who called and what language could they possibly speak?

•—•

My little pink room that held no phone yet: pink as a pencil's head, pink as an esophagus. The wicker chair where my mother rocked me, undisturbed, by the wan lamplight of the early years. There were roses on those walls—almost an imperative, instructing me how to be a daughter. Girls like frilly, delicate things (*don't they?*). The doll with the velvet dress and tatted shawl who kept watch from a corner shelf—whose tiny porcelain nail beds we painted. Girls always do as they're told (*don't they?*). The bed made every morning, the still-warm pajamas slipped down the chute, the hairbrush and powder puff on the vanity table, stubborn and silent, in the room where no phones rang, not yet.

My mother had a French telephone on her nightstand, ivory and gold. She conducted important business on the bed with her shoes off, her steno pad poised. (*Can I put you down for a casserole?*) (*Flower-arranging is set for the morning program.*) (*Just a small donation would be much appreciated.*) Her voice was never demure, always an imperative. I crouched in the hall, listening to the rotary spin, picturing the seven numbers flying like a carnival ride at the fair. She worked late into the night sometimes, for Delta Kappa Gamma and the Garden Club, for Bingo and Bunco and AAUW. I thought if I listened long enough I might learn the secrets of ladyhood: how to speak only like you mean it, polite and precise, never wavering. Even a question is never a question. A request only cloaks a demand.

Sometimes I fell asleep and my father would find me, crumpled against the grandfather clock he had come to wind. His back was not so bad yet that he couldn't lift me, cradle me in his arms as he carried me back to bed. "You're going to be a little wilted flower tomorrow," he'd say, not quite scold, pulling the mauve sheets up to my nose, then the quilt like a patchwork blush, a wave of cotton. In the room without inlets or outlets, I slept like the pink pearl I was, soon to erase everything.

•—•

Erasure: the sound of a telephone ringing in an empty house. A request becoming a demand becoming disappointment. The phone rings 5 (*polite*), 7 (*precise*), 9, 11 (*peeved*) times, almost giving up, then 12 (*resigned*), the quiet afterward like a sigh. It's a mystery now, words unspoken but held suspended, pearls in the groove of a tongue.

Sometimes you could hear the phone ringing as you pulled up in the station wagon, your mother hurrying out of the car, fumbling with the bags and keys, rushing inside to pick up… and nothing, just the echo of a *click*. She stood there a few moments, earpiece in hand, warbling *hello?* into the silence, as if the question, the repetition, could be an incantation, recalling the caller from oblivion. The house vibrated in the aftermath of a missed call; the rooms, after all, had heard the insistent ring, and they'd inclined toward the phone, wondering. They would have picked up, if they could, would have taken a message.

Messages written on the chalkboard in the kitchen. Coming home from a night out, you automatically swiveled your head to the chalkboard to see if anyone had called, if anyone wanted you. But those messages were imprecise: *Kevin called.* You imagined your mother talking to the boy, saying *May I take a message?* like the career secretary she'd been. She was an expert at answering the phone, had just the right inflections, the accent of professional courtesy. And even those simple words made you blush: the thought of your boyfriend's voice in her ear, and then her careful transcription in chalk on the board. She couldn't say what he wanted, couldn't have really known.

You often declined to go out, instead sitting by the telephone—no, not *by* it, but as close as possible, the phone in your lap—willing it to ring. You didn't dare move, didn't even go to the bathroom, because what if you missed it? That jangly bell summoning you, and you lunged to get it (*I've got it!*), your voice cracking with panic and hope. If it wasn't the person you expected, you yelled *I have to keep this line open!* and hung up, still waiting. Once you got the call you wanted, *if* it finally arrived, you stayed on the line for hours, speaking in various positions: sitting up, lying down, rolled onto your back, your hand caressing the cord.

Your house had one line, two phones, so sometimes you heard the surreptitious click of someone picking up—intentionally or by accident—eavesdropping on your intimate pauses. Your mother or your brother might butt in to say they needed the line (*get off the phone!*), and you hissed *okay! Just a minute!* And you occupied the line, the only line, a few moments longer to say your awkward goodbyes.

You remember the sound of a busy signal: that loud, brash, staccato buzz—almost angry, indignant, saying: *you can't get through.* If you were desperate, if the line had been busy for hours, you could ask the operator to break in, an emergency, and the speakers—your boyfriend and another girl?—heard the distant, officious voice of the operator telling them to *get off the line.* And there you'd be, embarrassed, with your non-emergency. What was worse? The busy signal—signifying life, someone home, but unconcerned about you? Or the phone ringing in an empty house, the echo of your insistence (*pick up, pick up*) to answer?

•—•

It's a mystery now, how the world your parents loved is lost, how the world you think you love is empty, shallow as water slipping through the lips of Puget Sound. They keep eavesdropping on your heart (*how they do this, you'll never know*), then breaking in with their loud, concerned voices: *So many false prophets*, they warn. *So many paths to perdition!*

Your father has two telephones in his basement office: an old brown rotary for home, a slick new push-button for work. *Two lines.* Plugged into their respective wall ports, the phones sit side by side like rivals, or worse—married people who no longer touch each other. You envy the way your father has another life where he is important, the glimpses you have of it: graph paper, a swivel chair, a desk light that bends to various positions, a black-handled magnifying lens.

Sometimes you play a game where he calls you on the home line from his work phone in the office. You stand at the top of the stairs in the kitchen by the big yellow phone, the one you call *the mothership*. Mostly, it belongs to your mother. This phone is big like a blimp, yellow like a submarine. You love answering this phone, stretching the cord long as a jump rope, straddling it, then trying on inflections the way some girls try on shoes: the interrogative, the imperative, softening your voice to a whisper or making it whistle-sharp.

Your parents say one day boys are going to call asking for you, wanting to take you out on dates, to restaurants and dances—but you don't believe them. Your parents also say you must never call boys, regardless of your generation's lax morals, its desperate search for *quick fixes* and *instant gratification*. None of this means anything to you yet. You like to play with Shawn across the street, so you call him sometimes in secret. Mostly, his mother answers. Her name is Adele, which reminds you of *addled.* You can hear sadness in the spaces between her words. She is all line breaks, like a slow, disconsolate poem.

Your own mother intercepts you at the threshold. "Who was that you were talking to?" You tell her you and Shawn are going to play tennis, you and Shawn are going to climb trees. You tell her yes, *he* called *you.* What you don't tell is that you and Shawn are going to double back to his family room and prank-call all the neighbors for hours—until the officious operator cuts in to report, "We've had some complaints associated with this number." You will roll on your backs, howling with laughter. You will close the White Pages, toss them back on the shelf. Everything is still funny then, and for no good reason. Even when you grow up, you will never touch each other.

•—•

The Yellow Pages arrived every year, predictable as migration: that heavy *thump* on the threshold, as if something had crawled to your porch to die. Whether you wanted it or not—if there had been big changes or none at all—you had to drag the directory inside and find somewhere to put it. For some reason, your mother kept the old books for a while, stacking them under the counter like building blocks (*you never know*)… Maybe it seemed a shame to toss out something so big, so substantial—something that wanted only to be of use.

Whenever you needed anything—from an auto mechanic to a zoo—you pulled out the Yellow Pages and thumbed through the slick listings, trying to discern from the language and format of the entries which company might serve you best. You always wondered about the one-line listings in pale, non-bolded font: they announced themselves hardly at all, gave you no reason to call. These companies nestled like secrets between the display ads—loud promotions that held pictures of smiling tradesmen kneeling with their children, proclaiming *Family Business! Serving you since 1959*—and for that reason alone you wanted to call the quiet ones and see who might answer, what they'd have to say for themselves.

Public phone booths used to have the Yellow Pages dangling by a chain, protected by thick, black plastic covers. When you tried to use these directories, they thwarted your efforts; you had to twist and turn to get them to open and lie flat. You had to find a nickel, a dime, a quarter, rummaging in your pocket or purse, your elbows banging against the glass. You had to hold the phone wedged between ear and shoulder while you deposited change and kept your finger pointed to the number you wanted to call. You often dropped your coins. You had to disregard those people standing outside the booth, peering in, waiting impatiently for their turn. Watching you there, boxed in—private but public, your need for help on display.

Once, in a phone booth at a beach park, you kept a long line of people waiting for a half hour while you cried to a friend. *I don't know what to do*, you repeated, clutching the receiver, keeping your gaze narrowed to the metal shelf dusty with grit, studded with chewed gum. Someone had stolen the Yellow Pages; the chain dangled empty. People grumbled, and one boy banged on the glass. They thought you were addled, or simply rude. But you had to hold onto the voice at the other end of the line. The voice talked you down, told you to take deep breaths, move one foot at a time to a café where you would eat a bowl of brown rice and vegetables with peanut sauce. The store next to the café sold crystals and amulets. You might find something there to see you through into your next life.

Whenever you drove long-distance—another broken relationship funneling out behind you—you noticed every phone booth you passed, or every opportunity for a phone booth, exits blinking by like pauses in your sadness. Every phone booth setting off a ping in your chest, igniting that desire to call, to hear a voice one more time, to get some *closure.* But you could never have enough change to bridge these particular distances, these breaks in the line. You'd need to call collect, and what if no one accepted the charges?

•—•

And then there were calling cards, cheap and pre-paid from Costco. Times were changing. Even change was changing. Coins no longer jangled in your purse or pocket. You had the card, see. It was sleek and white with a silver stripe you scratched off like a lottery ticket. You called your parents with it—from the beige standard-issue dorm phone, from the greasy payphone after work at the mall, from your first apartment on the push-button receiver with numbers that glowed in the dark.

Flash to an episode of *Matlock* where Conrad, the chief PI, breaks into a suspicious efficiency. There he finds an empty room, a gritty floor, three Yellow Pages stacked askew. "What do people do on a stakeout?" he muses aloud, following the phone cord to a rotary on the windowsill. You can still hear the echo of his boots in that barren space, still remember the trick that delighted you: how he paused to lift the phone book on top, then dropped it so the pages splayed wide. "You order a lot of pizza," he answers himself. And sure enough, the book yields its secrets like a primed confessor, falling open to the food section—Italian eateries, the bold-stroke slogan *WE DELIVER!*

You were lucky no one could do that with your mind: rifle through your repeated wishes, peer inside the little jukebox of longing where you spent the most time. You had become so good at being quiet by your college days, tamping down and tucking in, collecting sadness like pennies in a well. Everyone remarked how your voicemail greeting didn't even sound like you, so you replaced it with music, then learned how to screen your calls.

You could make them wait, but you couldn't escape them—their questions bridging the distance you had built: book by book and mile by mile. *What are you eating? What are you learning?* (And under those questions nestled the real ones: *What is your weight? What are your grades?*) It wasn't until the night you didn't call back at all that they decided to drive north. All night the little green numbers glowed on your phone alone. You were glowing, too, until the urgent ring, your father's voice cutting in like too-bright light through morning curtains. "Why are you not sleeping in your own bed?" he demanded to know. "What do you have to say for yourself?"

•—•

"How did you find me?" I asked, voice still croaked with sleep, or not sleep but the aftermath of sex. I squiggled into my pants, couldn't talk to my father while naked from the waist down. We'd known the minute the bedside phone jangled in the white apartment that it was my father calling, the ring insistent and angry as his voice.

And, of course, that had never been the right question.

There were years, I know, when my parents couldn't find me. I moved away to college, lived in an old Victorian house with ten other people. I called from a payphone on a Berkeley street—surrounded by the scents of falafel and patchouli—and said I wanted to come home. *Hang in there*, my mother said, but I know she must have cried when she hung up. After college, I drifted from state to state, and I remember no phone calls then, though there must have been: truncated calls, where I hid all my secrets, said everything was fine. I lived in a campground, lived in a trailer, lived on strangers' couches. I never had a phone. I must have called from various booths, must have slipped once and said, *all I want is to go home*, and my mother asked, *where is home?*

That has always been the right question.

When I rented my first apartment, with my own phone, I bought a little cassette answering machine. It took quite a while to record the outgoing message, to time all the clicks, to figure out what I wanted to say and to say it just right. I erased and erased, ended up finally with the officious *You've reached*… and *Please leave a message after the beep.*

It became a reflex to look for the light of messages as soon as I walked in the door, the way I had swiveled my head to the chalkboard in my mother's kitchen. And a reflex too: the glad lift when the machine blinked its green light, the heavy drop at nothing. I still pushed the button to hear *you have no new messages*, just to make sure. I rewound the tiny cassette and played old messages, just to have other voices in the room. My mother. A friend. An official from school.

Once, an obscene phone call, a message under the cheerful green light: *I want to fuck your brains out.* The man's voice gravelly in the throat, gritty in the room. Even then, I thought it strange that the man would leave a message, would wait so politely for the beep. I played it twice, to make sure I'd heard right, then erased it. You could do that then: erase what you didn't want. Could watch the tape go back to its own beginning and start again, start again, until it broke.

•—•

In the beginning was the gray, and it was called weather. In the beginning was the bell, and it was called school and church and dinner. Always a summons to one thing, away from another, and just as we were settling in, time to change again.

We had seven phones in our home by the time I was grown, and one would always ring first, sounding an alarm. The others followed, like rivals or worse—a family that yammered constantly with nothing substantial to say.

One year we got an answering machine. My mother said they were all the rage. After that, when a call came during mealtime, we sat stiff as mannequins: *one ring, two rings, three rings, four*. We waited for my father's canned voice to rise up through the vents, sweep across the kitchen floor: "We are unable to answer the phone at this time. Please leave your name, number, and the reason for your call, and we'll return it just as soon as we can."

Before long, my mother never wanted to answer the phone, its ring suddenly presumptuous, an imposition on her time. Instead, she ran to the landing, crouched on the stairs—static, her body silent, as though the caller could hear her if she moved.

"I know you're there!" her friends sighed, echoing each other. "Pick up!" my father insisted. "I need to talk to you."

Soon, she forbade us to answer the phone, even if we were *expecting a call*. "If it's so important, they will leave a message," she hissed. "And if it's not important, why are we wasting our time?"

Eventually, my mother proposed a code: let the phone ring twice, hang up, wait ten seconds, redial. Then, and only then, would the person at home lift the receiver, clutch it in his sticky palm, press it to her addled ear.

I didn't use this code the last time I called my mother. Were her knees too sore to crouch? Did she lean against the wall instead, steady herself on the railing? It was still my father's voice that followed the beep, but did I detect a waver, the deep moon of sound slowly waning?

What I might have said: *You aren't home to me anymore.* (Too harsh.) *We're history.* (Too curt.)

What I did say, clear as a bell: "I love her." Were they listening as I dangled on the line?

•—•

Are you listening? Words dangle midair as they pass from child to child: a mouth to an ear, the head inclined, a smile of attention. Then the head swivels to the next in line, words already morphing into new meaning or nonsense. How many children? As many as you want there to be. They line up and shuffle in place, already giggling. The last one delivers the message in its mutant form, and laughter somersaults through them.

The man in the Verizon commercial struts from place to place, phone pressed to his ear. *Can you hear me now? Can you hear me now?* Yes, we hear each other everywhere. Words whiz through the air, from ear to ear—imperative, interrogative—disembodied as the moon. We overhear: *where are you?* We catch: *love you.*

Thousands of *love you's* before the phones click off. *Love* without the *I.*

Before Alexander invented the telephone, he worked with deaf children (Helen Keller was one of his pupils). His own mother was deaf, and his future wife, Mabel, came to him first as a student. She wrote: *Have no recollection of hearing except of a soft low sound I always called the singing of the frogs.* Bell invented the telephone for her, that they might speak. She could already see his love in his lips, but not feel it in her ears. His rival, Elisha, and his "harmonic telegraphs" couldn't reach far enough, could convey only music. Music, in this case, was not enough.

But the first words over the telephone line are not directed to Bell's wife. His assistant becomes the recipient of this oft-repeated, often misquoted line: *Mr. Watson, come here, I want to see you.* Or perhaps the only intelligible word: *want.*

Imagine: all language is code, and we spend our lives on the line, waiting for the right voice to reach us. A voice we can understand. And every message, decoded, means: *I love.*

Toys

I.

What would you expect to find? Raggedy Ann, certainly, and her lesser-known counterpart, Raggedy Andy. Crayola crayons. Mr. Potato Head and Baby Doll and Slinky. Candy Land (*oh yes*). Your old Etch A Sketch, screen marred with erased images of the past. To date, 74 toys have been inducted into the National Toy Hall of Fame in Rochester, New York, chosen through these criteria:

> ***Icon-status:*** *The toy is widely recognized, respected, and remembered.*
> ***Longevity****: The toy is more than a passing fad and has enjoyed popularity over multiple generations.*
> ***Discovery****: The toy fosters learning, creativity, or discovery through play.*
> ***Innovation****: The toy profoundly changed play or toy design.*

Here's something you didn't imagine: Cardboard Box. Not a mechanized cardboard box, or a decorated cardboard box, or a box hiding bits and pieces of a puzzle. Just a box: brown, with four flaps, about the size of a microwave oven. Or another, the size of a refrigerator. Or perhaps one as small as a shoebox. Any plain box will do: open, flaps flapping, empty of all content. Cardboard boxes came into use in the nineteenth century: a lightweight and reusable alternative to wooden crates. Once emptied, they could be flattened and stored away. Cardboard boxes were meant to be strictly utilitarian, but children always know better; they know the best use for something empty is to fill it with their own bodies. They know that emptiness is simply space waiting to be transformed.

Remember? It could be Christmas or Hanukkah or your birthday. It could be the aftermath of a delivery, your parents preoccupied with whatever new shiny thing had arrived. It could be a surprise waiting for you in an alleyway: Cardboard Box, set out with the trash.

Cardboard Box beckons. You squeeze yourself inside, smell the residue of styrofoam, a few packing peanuts wafting at your feet. You feel the dry, thick-but-thin walls mold your body to a new shape. You become a present waiting to be opened.

Cardboard Box becomes a house, a cave, a castle. Cardboard Box becomes a car, a rocket, a train. Cardboard Box tips over and becomes a fort, a refuge. Who are you inside this box? According to the National Toy Hall of Fame, *Inside a big cardboard box, a child is transported to a world of his or her own, one where anything is possible.*

II.

Inside the box, you can become anyone, change your name to Stephanie Smith or Mary Ann Johnson. "But they're so ordinary!" your parents protest when you present your list of alternative names. Maybe that's the greatest secret of the cardboard box: its capacity to embrace the most ordinary contents.

You aren't sure you're ready for exceptional responsibility: the only child, the only grandchild, the only niece. The box is the size of a child's playhouse and stands beside the playhouse it formerly contained. When your friend comes to visit, he converts your plastic cottage with window shutters, roll-out awnings, and a painted tulip border into a workshop that resembles his father's. He says he can hammer all day long. He wants you to pretend to make him a sandwich so he can just keep hammering on the imaginary workbench with the imaginary tool.

This isn't going to work for you. You don't practice vacuuming or dusting, organizing spices or folding laundry fresh from the line. You borrow your father's binoculars, practice crouching and holding impossibly still in preparation for your future life as a private eye.

Though it's true that your family wants you to be extraordinary—

gifted academically, prodigious on piano, a catalog model for JCPenney—such accomplishments must not come at the expense of being normal. They buy you classic, gender-specific toys now immortalized in the Hall of Fame: a baby doll you call Amy and a fashion doll someone else has already called Barbie. *Every baby doll… serves a special function in cultivating nurturing and parental roles in children*—except you never want to mother Amy. She becomes your sister instead, the one you long for but will never have. Let Amy play piano. Let Amy pose for pictures. You prop her in a cardboard corner with your schoolbooks, make her hold your imaginary periscope, test you on your spelling words.

Barbie, once charged with limiting girls' potential, went on to pursue many specialized careers, including dentist, paleontologist, and presidential candidate. *Even in demanding positions, though, Barbie retained her fashion sense.* You are not one of those girls who shave Barbie's head or remove it altogether. She is never your object of revenge. Instead, you leave her lonely on the basement stairs, beside the boxes that contain her dream house and her glow-in-the-dark canopy bed.

It's true there are other toys in the Hall of Fame you would have much preferred: Hot Wheels, Mr. Potato Head, a shiny red Radio Flyer. But you are content, for the most part, to lie flat on your belly, palms cupping your chin, watching the world and writing about it on a steno pad with a Ticonderoga pencil.

Next door, your friend keeps hammering away with sound effects and pounding motions. He rattles your box. He recounts his plans to build skyscrapers *that really scrape the sky*. At lunchtime, you call for Barbie to bring each of you a sandwich.

III.

I search the National Toy Hall of Fame for *my* doll, my namesake—Brenda the Nurse—but she's nowhere in sight. Where could she be? Maybe hard at work behind the scenes, saving the lives of other, more important toys.

Perhaps I made her up. But I seem to remember her so clearly: she lay flat and cool as a drugged princess in her plastic box, a case gussied up to look like a hospital. She wore a svelte black cape emblazoned with a red cross and a perky white nurse's cap tilted at a rakish angle. She clutched a cunning black doctor's bag in her tiny curved fingers, and I believed it held everything she would need in her day: stethoscope, tinted cylinders of pills, packets of Kleenex for her patients.

When my mother gave her to me—an unexpected gift, not part of a birthday or Hanukkah—I could tell she was pleased to have found something so perfect. Not that I had expressed any desire to be a nurse (my thoughts ran more to stewardess in those days, and I even sent away for a catalog from which one could order one's very own stewardess cap and sash). But rarely did I find my name among the racks of bicycle license plates or key chains at the drugstore, a deflation my mother had witnessed many times. To twirl the rack and look hopefully at the Bobbies and Bonnies and then to the Bruces, with no Brendas in between, felt almost like an annihilation, as if I didn't really exist.

As it turns out, my mother gave me "Brenda Bride," *not* Brenda the Nurse (of course, "bride" back then was considered a perfectly acceptable, perhaps even better, occupation for young girls to practice). She also gave me Sally Stewardess, and one of my friends got Nina the Nurse. Brenda came in a box that looked like a storybook house, the place of her occupation.

But I prefer to remember her as Brenda the Nurse, a doll with *purpose* beyond pleasing her man. I've never been a bride, after all, and could never be contained in such a cozy house. I want to remember my doppelgänger Brenda in her portable hospital, including an attic room where she slept on a cot (why she would live in such austerity, I don't know). The other rooms would be saved for work: a waiting room, an examination room. I imagined myself in soft-soled shoes, padding quietly down hallways, dispensing tender yet efficient smiles at every doorway, my head nodding demurely at anything a doctor said. And then I would go home to my attic room, where I would fall into my spartan bed, exhausted, and lay the cool metal of the stethoscope against my chest to count out the beats, my rhythm of being alive.

IV.

My mother had already decided I would become a doctor when I grew up. She liked the idea of the white coat, the prescription pad, my future heels clicking with feminine authority down the long, clean hospital hallways. Of course, the high salary and the cachet of saving lives could not be underestimated either.

"And the best way to meet a doctor is to be one yourself!" She winked at me in the rearview mirror.

I don't recall having an Elizabeth Blackwell doll, but I had a book that told the story of the first woman physician of the modern era. I liked Elizabeth Blackwell right away, which I suppose was the point of the gift. She taught women about their bodies, and she traveled around the world. She also avoided matrimony, which I found an intriguing idea. On this matter, my mother was conspicuously silent.

One year, Santa Claus left me a black medicine bag, familiar from movies in which bald, kindly doctors made house calls, touched the cheeks of fevered children, then promised their parents that everything would be all right. The trouble was, I didn't know any doctors in real life. I was rarely sick, and my mother took me only once to Dr. Kumasaka, whose name I repeated over and over: *ku-ma-sa-ka, ku-ma-sa-ka.* He was quiet and serious, with a bright light on his forehead and slender, ghostly hands. When he pricked my finger, he showed me the wild red of my blood. "It is only this color," he said, "after the air has touched it." Then he wrapped the small wound with a Snoopy Band-Aid, and I never saw him again.

Soon after, I removed the plastic syringes from my own kit, the mysterious bottle of tonic, even the stack of gauze pads and the tiny thermometer set precisely to 98.6. I stocked up instead on the tools of my own future trade—rumpled notebooks, erasable pens, a flashlight, a camera, and a magnifying lens. Nancy Drew was always with me, and Trixie Belden, too. Even the Hardy Boys had a place in my portable archive.

Are there really no books in the National Toy Hall of Fame? Are Alphabet Blocks and Scrabble the closest its curators came to priming a life for the sustained investigation of words? On Career Day in third grade, I stood in front of the class, opened the medicine bag, and revealed my treasures. "I'm going to be a detective," I explained, "and I'll also be writing mystery novels on the side."

In the back row, my mother's face sagged. She must have thought of stakeouts, donuts by the dozen, mussed hair, and bad grooming habits. Of the writing, she said only, "It won't be worth it unless you write for Hallmark or just like Danielle Steel."

V.

No books in the National Toy Hall of Fame? This must be an oversight! Are we ever more at play than when we crouch down inside a book? Isn't a book just as playful (full of play), and just as ready to be filled with a child's body, as Cardboard Box? Watch a child reading: she is no longer present in the ordinary, too-serious world.

I see the Game of Life occupies a place in this hallowed hall (though, now, my regard for this canonical display has diminished just a tad). *One of the best-selling games of all time, Life has also been translated into at least 20 languages.* It was one of the first "3-D" board games, with its upright, movable pieces and its integrated spinner. The television commercial promised that *You will learn about life when you play the Game of Life!* Even Art Linkletter said so.

We used to drag this battered box onto the kitchen table, fold out the game board, choose our mode of transportation: for me, a practical roadster with slots ready for the tiny, upright plastic driver, spouse, and kids. Pink for girls, blue for boys. You had many choices to make in the Game of Life. Business or college? Children? How many? Insurance? Do you take risks or follow the winding path on a predictable trajectory?

The spinner spins, lands where it may. I move my jalopy from one square to the next, fill it with people who can face only one direction. I buy no insurance. At some point, the Game of Life becomes tedious, and you want to skip out, go back to your room with a book. *A Wrinkle in Time*, say, or *Stranger in a Strange Land.* Yes, that's it. You take this book with you wherever you go, even in the car, with Mom and Dad sitting immovable in their appointed slots, staring straight ahead into their future.

VI.

We had the Game of Life, but we never played it, not even once. I have my hunch as to why. My father always said, "Too many choices can be dangerous. That's why God left us a guidebook—so we wouldn't presume to decide."

Free will leads to sin, remember? Choice is just temptation in disguise.

I was once a girl in lacy socks, then a teenaged Eve in appropriate attire—but look how badly she bungled that business in the Garden. Dragged Adam into it, too. And everyone knew you couldn't leave me alone with a box of Jujyfruits. Imagine the mess I'd make if the Tree of Knowledge of Good and Evil were to sprout beneath my bedroom window. *You're going to college. You're getting married. You're having two children, a boy and a girl.* I never heard an *or*. No one spoke the language of *maybe* where I came from.

My parents promised to help me with my down payment, though. "You'll live right here in our neighborhood," my father said. "That way, your mother can help you with the children."

We played other games instead, some since inducted into the National Toy Hall of Fame—games that didn't threaten to undermine the patriarchy or contradict God's word. Marbles, for instance. My father brought me a wooden box. The lid didn't lift but slid slowly, intensifying the suspense. Inside, I found dozens of small, hard balls of colored glass. Hundreds, perhaps. They looked brand new, and

I soon learned that this was because he had polished them religiously for years in preparation for the day he would pass the box on to me.

"Someday," my father declared, arranging a circle of string on the living room rug, "you will pass these marbles to your own daughter, your own son." For him, I was both in one. I must have been pretty young then, still wearing those lacy socks and something pink jutting out of my head. "But what if I don't have any children?" I asked. Everyone knew about them, after all—the disgusting messes they made, the relentless questions they raised. I was an expert on everything wrong with children.

"Don't you *ever*—" he said it louder than he meant, and harsher, too, "—say that again."

VII.

Have you lost your marbles?! my brother would say to me, gleefully, the "are" sound of *marbles* elongated so the word itself seemed marbled, clicking and clacking through his sinuses. Always followed by a snort, then his hand reaching in to tickle my ribs. *Have you*, he said, tickling harder, *lost your marrrrrrbles?*, until I shrieked in a puzzling combination of pleasure and pain. I didn't really understand; I had no marbles to begin with. Well, I had one marble: an agate, milky blue swirled with white. I kept it in a little plastic box, along with a feathered barrette, a tiny key to a lost diary, and a mood ring.

Do you remember mood rings? That round oval of mysterious, prophetic stone nestled in a cheap tin setting? The stone contained liquid crystal that changed color depending on the wearer's skin temperature, this fluctuation supposedly correlating to the true level of one's happiness. Originally, jewelers crafted the settings of real silver or gold, and the rings sold for hundreds of dollars in upscale stores like Bonwit Teller. But the demand for a piece of jewelry that exposes your inner self must not have escalated among the upper classes; the market trended steadily downward to the drugstore variety of consumer—mainly children, who idly fingered impulse buys at the checkout counter or gazed at trinkets jumbled behind the domed glass of a vending machine.

I wore the mood ring on my left ring finger like a wedding band or engagement ring. I liked the heavy feel of it against my knuckle, the way the stone took up more room than it should have, and I glanced at it often. Each ring came with a color chart that correlated every color with an emotion: the blood red of Nervous, the burnt umber of Harassed, the yellow of Mixed Emotions.

As children, we have no words to describe what bubbles within us; our bodies must do it for us. My mood ring often stayed black—did I feel nothing? Even now I have cold hands—but sometimes it strayed into a dirty gold or the surprise of teal. Did I ever get Happy or Lucky? How about the green light of Romantic? Perhaps only when I ran.

VIII.

My mood ring came from the Southgate Roller Rink: a stray quarter slipped into the silver slot and then a plastic egg slid through the polished chute, bearing one of four kinds of treasure. People were just beginning to pair off. At least three times a night was a Couples' Skate, and that's how you knew who the *friends* were, who the *more-than-friends*.

Inexplicably, I had a steady boyfriend for all of fourth grade and half of fifth. Like everyone else, we wanted to be older. Like everyone else, we didn't know how. The girls in my class thought Lee was too pretty and normal for me, destined for titles like *Team Captain* and *Homecoming King*. They weren't wrong. But back then, we wore matching friendship bracelets we wove ourselves, and when he asked me to slow-skate, I put my sweaty palm inside his sweaty palm, the way our parents set their cars on cruise control. It was all so easy and automatic, lacing our fingers and swaying under the soft lights to something like Debbie Gibson's "Lost in Your Eyes."

All the while, though, the ring pinched between my knuckles, tighter and tighter, until it drew blood. The color had always been one denoting Romantic, Happy, or Lucky. But later, when Lee pressed me against the wall by the snack bar, the way all the pretty boys pressed all the normal girls, I got flustered and couldn't breathe. A stranger flashed her inhaler at me, but I didn't have asthma or even allergies. When I looked down at the ring, it had turned yellow, unmistakably: the color of Mixed Emotions. Not long, then, before I threw that ring away.

Roller skates belong in the National Toy Hall of Fame, so I'm not surprised to find them there. Ditto skateboards, Big Wheels, and bicycles. Until we could drive, these were the best ways we had of getting around. But what about staying put or drawing closer, learning to share an intimate space? I wanted to talk to people all day long, but I was growing more and more afraid to touch them. Even casual contact—passing a pencil or hovering too close in a line—might be misconstrued. And what of the girl in the locker room, from the high-school swim team, who threw her wet hair so hard it whipped the air between us: "What are you, a lesbian or something?" I never went back to that pool.

The mood ring chart makes me think of Twister, which was inducted into the Hall of Fame in 2015. First introduced in 1966 by Milton Bradley, Twister was not an instant hit. Then, someone in PR made a last-ditch pitch to *The Tonight Show*. After Johnny Carson and Eva Gabor contorted themselves to laughter and rousing cheers, the game sold out everywhere. No store could keep it in stock.

Maybe this is what all toys do: grant their players some essential permission. What if I unfolded the slippery white mat on the dorm room floor and waved to my neighbors; if the whole east wing of Harstad Hall—girls in slippery white socks and leggings and messy buns without bangs—were suddenly stretching beyond their reach; if girls were falling all over each other, roaring with laughter, and I was one of them? What if, for once, no one worried where she would land?

Heat Index

Alcohol

In the sixteenth century, shipping companies often paid sailors in rations of rum. The sailors (always wary of the bosses) learned to test if they were being ripped off by pouring samples of the liquor on small piles of gunpowder and setting them on fire. If the gunpowder ignited, it "proved" the rum hadn't been watered down. If not—well, then there was hell to pay. From this, we get our current system of alcohol proofs: 100 proof (50 percent alcohol), 80 proof (40 percent), and so on. When my boyfriend drank, he preferred 100-proof vodka. We didn't need gunpowder to prove its efficacy, to make everything around us explode.

Ardor

The word "ardor" stems from the Latin *ardor*, which means "heat" or "burning." It's come to mean a fiery passion most likely short-lived. Flames that burn hot burn out, they say. Yet when we're in the throes of it, ardor masquerades as love—wants to be the steady burn of hardwood rather than the flash fire of kindling.

Bikram

This style of yoga takes its name from founder Bikram Choudhury, a controversial figure who claims his series of 26 Hatha postures restored him to full mobility after a disabling accident in his youth. Critics insist this story has not been verified. Bikram studios, of which thousands now exist worldwide, are heated to a minimum of 104 degrees to mimic the climate in India. One paradox of such high temperatures is that they aid in deepening each stretch, but they also deplete the body completely. At a certain point, your muscles become loose, hyper-flexible, but you become so dehydrated and light-headed that you are barely able to move. At Bikram Yoga Harlem, the teacher is a hairless, shiny man in a Speedo whose rib cage ripples like a waterfall. He takes the towel from my hand when I attempt to wrap it around my ankle. "Use the heat instead," he says. "Bend into it. There are no modifications allowed in Bikram."

Blush

I've been watching (over and over) a video that's gone viral on Facebook. A high-school girl is filming her classmates one by one; she frames them in her lens, then says: "I'm taking pictures of things I find beautiful." These teenagers have hair dyed orange, piercings in their noses; some are transgender; some have acne and braces. All of them look neutral or wary at first, dressed in a way that shows great attention to persona. Lots of makeup. Tortured hair. And then, at the word "beautiful," each face blooms in unguarded pleasure. They blush, the capillaries of their skin dilating with heat. They put their hands to their mouths. Some begin to cry.

Boiling Point

Sometimes called the "saturation temperature," it's the degree of heat required to vaporize a liquid. Water boils at 100 degrees Celsius, 212 Fahrenheit. I have to take the chemistry teacher's word for it, since I can never make the corresponding equation come out right. When he asks me to stay after class, I plead poetry as my defense for poor performance. "Poets aren't empiricists," I explain. "We're interested in describing more than proving." It must take a tremendous amount of self-control for Mr. Nowak not to roll his eyes. His own boiling point is set higher than most adults I know. "You see, I'd rather describe the sound the tea kettle makes when she reaches that heat than work the numbers to explain her whistle-song."

Can't take the

Harry S. Truman is thought to have coined the phrase as early as 1942. Known as a plain-spoken president, he reportedly told his White House staff not to quibble over their appointments: "I'll stand by [you], but if you can't take the heat, get out of the kitchen." During long Pennsylvania winters, we always sought refuge in the kitchen, baking all day or simply heating the cast-iron skillet inside the oven—to deepen its seasoning, we said, but really to warm our hands. In Florida, when temperatures dropped into the 40s, we tried to turn on the heat, but nothing happened. A quick call to maintenance explained the problem: "This building isn't wired for heat," the super said. "Given how rarely it's needed, management decided it wasn't worth the expense."

Dead

When I ran track, I tried to come in second because I thought the red ribbon was prettier than the blue. I'd match my opponent stride for stride, then pause a second on the final step so she could split the streamer at the finish line. Soon, though, the competition stiffened: twelve runners instead of six, the fearsome gun instead of the pleasant whistle. I moved to the back of the pack. A contender no longer, and my mother cried from the stands, "You're dead in the water out there!"

Desert

Once upon a time a fair maid lived with an evil prince in a trailer by an enchanted lake. This lake sprung up in the middle of the desert: sapphire-blue water against fiery red rocks. The water was cold and deep, held ghosts of drowned junipers and coyotes. Sometimes, at night, the maiden could hear cries of Anasazi women reach her from thousands of years away. One day, the evil prince took her out in a motor boat and drove her deep into an isolated side canyon. She had little food and water. She had a tent and a sleeping bag. He left her there to have what he called a *vision quest.* By day the heat grew steadily, enveloped her in its embrace. A dry heat. The water lapped against the shore, but she didn't dare go in. A raven traced a cat's cradle against the sky. Called her a new name. Wanted her to be transformed.

Discussion

When he told me he was leaving, things got a little *heated.* I repeated the word *why?*, my question marks growing loud and harsh. Our words had friction, threw sparks. It felt like arson. We lived in a log home in the middle of almost-nowhere, surrounded by woods. It wouldn't have taken much to start a wildfire.

Exhaustion

What comes after "heat cramps" but before "heat stroke"—this mezzanine of heavy sweat, rapid pulse, the body overheating the way car engines do. Caused by prolonged exposure to sun, too much exertion at high temperatures, not enough water. Even Jacuzzis and saunas can be culprits if you stay in long enough. Every September I ran the high school jogathon on the hottest day of the year. Sister Rosemary brought her sun umbrella to the track. Other teachers drank lemonade and fanned themselves with packets: our math homework and essay exams. In the single hour, I could do six miles, but I wanted to reach seven. Think of all those pledges—one dollar a mile, five dollars, ten. Think of all those silly girls who wore visors, took water breaks, chewed on ice. Think of all those girls who shamed themselves by walking. Not me. I wouldn't stop, even when Sister Rosemary suggested I was "dangerously red." Every year I missed the award ceremony. Home in bed—an ice pack on my head and feet, the mercury relentless in its rise.

Fever

The body fights fire with fire. In response to inflammation, the hypothalamus resets the body's core temperature to burn out intruders. The hypothalamus sits deep within the brain, manning the controls. It monitors signals from throughout the body and regulates just about anything: thirst, hunger, mood, carnal desire. It craves *homeostasis*, the status quo. Imagine it hunched over a switchboard, directing input and output—a little bit here, a little bit there. It remains cool. It never takes a coffee break or chats at the vending machines. It never gets out of hand.

Geothermal

Once upon a time there was a girl who lived in a valley where hot water burbled up from underground. She was a very pretty girl, but not the fairest in the land. Still, she worked hard every day: weeding the garden, cleaning the hot tubs, answering phones at the front desk and making reservations for honored guests who wished to partake of the magical waters. She was a gatekeeper; occasionally she needed to escort an ogre from the property. She lived in a shack with a man who was not a prince. But when she disrobed in the bathhouse at dawn, the waters claimed they loved her. Water poured over her neck, her arms, her breasts. Her skin grew soft, luminous. She became a queen, a woman who glowed with power.

Global

Some believe in it and some don't. But according to climate scientists, it's not a question of warming, but of excess. The extremes continue to become more extreme: blizzards, hurricanes, temperatures at either end of the spectrum. Like the proverbial frog in the pot of water on the stove, we won't notice until it's too late. We'll be *cooked.*

"Heat" (Drama)

Something about how the police *are* "the heat" or criminals "feel the heat" whenever the police come near. The plot is hard to follow. In the 1995 film, Robert De Niro plays a cunning thief; Al Pacino plays a savvy cop. Maybe "cunning" and "savvy" are really synonyms, but a villain answers to one, a hero to the other? Words are more interesting to me than men. They are currently running in a dead heat with women. I go to high school with only girls. I dream about only girls. When a girl and I watch this movie together on VHS, she laughs. "I don't think you can even tell those old Italian dudes apart!"

Hell

All we know is that it's supposed to be hot—a raging furnace, a lake of fire. Later, we learn "Hell hath no fury like a woman scorned," an idiom not to be confused with "She's hotter than Hell." Perhaps Hell, like God, is in the details. Or perhaps anger and attraction are closer than cousins after all. Maybe we don't always want the heat of wanting. Maybe it burns us up to burn for the beloved this way. Anne Carson writes, "Love, as you know, is a harrowing event." *Hellish,* we call it, the aching descent into desire.

Hot & cold

Like fever and chills of the heart. So many strong verbs: to waver; to oscillate or vacillate; to toggle between possibles or straddle a line. More recently and politically: to flip-flop. The phrase evokes mood rings and pendulums, the fickle lover and the bar room tease. Perhaps even the Magic 8-Ball. From the Greek, *peripeteia*: a reversal of intention or outcome. A twist, a recursion. In other words, as it's often construed: to be wishy-washy, to send mixed signals, to give false hope, to change—that most daring maneuver—your mind.

Hot & heavy

I've read that committed couples are only "hot and heavy" for the first 18 months, the length of time it takes to secure each other's trust. But what about Eliot's "lifetime burning in every moment"? What about the blue flame that leaps up in a lover's throat each time she remembers the death in "death do us part"? My father had a blank gag book called *Sex after Fifty*. My mother's friends joked about pressing "pause on men" at menopause. Viagra commercials make me blush—a man and woman holding hands in separate bathtubs on the beach. I blush for their nakedness, their vulnerability, the silliness of this scenario. Still, I know physical passion deepens other kinds of intimacy. It has been nineteen years for me. I feel only more, not less. I think awareness of mortality is the ultimate aphrodisiac.

Hot & spicy

My father-in-law buys "Slap Ya Mama" by the case. He pours the sauce into chili, the seasoning onto scrambled eggs. My brother-in-law has been known to order the napalm nachos at Toot's, a chain restaurant in Tennessee. If you can eat the whole plate, your order is free, but you may need a quart of milk to calm your stomach down. By the time he is three, my nephew demands Tabasco in his soup, cries for cherry peppers on his grilled cheese. Perhaps there is a "some like it hot" gene that runs in families. My spouse douses every entrée with Sriracha. Our pantry shelves are lined with green-tipped bottles sporting the proud white rooster design. Meanwhile, I coax mild jalapeños from under my beans, slip them discreetly onto her plate.

In

When an animal is ready to mate, she's *in heat.* Her hormones put her into estrus—eggs plumping up, uterus thickening, all cylinders firing. Breeding females are called *bitches*, but it's not meant as an insult. I once fostered a nine-month-old shepherd as she gave birth to eight puppies. She'd gone into heat as a stray, and from the looks of the litter, more than one male sniffed her out. Though I knew it was all simply biological—that the dog, Becky, wouldn't feel any shame—I wept when I thought of her on the streets, beset by males, trapped.

Index

It turns out that the old adage "It's not the heat, it's the humidity" is true. The heat index, created by weatherman George Winterling in 1978, calculates how poorly sweat will evaporate in humid conditions, thus creating the *perception* that you're hotter than you actually are. He first called it the "humiture." He predicted the landfall of Hurricane Dora in Jacksonville, Florida in 1964—the early years of televised weather reports. George was innocuously good-looking, in the way of meteorologists. Someone you could trust: photogenic for the camera—blond hair, a craggy nose, bright eyes—but not what you could call *hot.*

Journey to the Center of the Earth

In the Jules Verne novel, Professor Otto Lidenbrock, his nephew Axel, and their guide Hans descend one volcano in Iceland and eventually resurface through another volcano in Italy. Even with my limited understanding of world geography, I find this premise ludicrous. "But isn't it exciting," my father prods, "all the adventures they have underground?" I hate the way adventure stories are always written by men about other men and boys. I am a girl who wants to have adventures, too. "It would be more exciting if there were a girl in there—doing something," I say. "Doing anything."

Masala Chai

The word "chai" means, simply, tea. But often, here in the west, when we order a *chai* we really mean "Masala Chai," that particular combination of black tea, cinnamon, cardamom, ginger, and black peppercorns. We dilute it with steamed milk and honey. When you take the first sip—gingerly, because it's hot—the spices ignite first your lips, then your tongue, finally warming the belly, where your *chi* simmers. My yoga teacher, Ruby, makes it with coconut milk and organic sugar as a treat for our hard work. We hover around her at the tea station, glowing from our exertions.

Miami

In winter, all of South Florida revolves around the Miami Heat. Their games are broadcast at every taco shack along the beach, in every bar and probably every boardroom, too. Boys wear oversized jerseys that fit like dresses. Swaddled to their knees, it becomes difficult to shoot, let alone leap to the hoop like Dwyane or LeBron. When we first moved here, I thought I was seeing signs for a Pentecostal church, a holy white halo filled with righteous fire. "Naw, that's the logo for the Miami Heat," a Super Fan touting the image on his t-shirt explained. "And if you think that's neat, you should see Burnie, the team's mascot." Then, as if it was something people said every day: "He's great. He's an anthropomorphic fireball."

Of the moment

Adrenaline is a primal drug. Whoever designed us figured we'd need a little boost to help us spring into action against threat. Saber-toothed tigers, say, or an unfamiliar man bearing a club. Our bodies actually sense danger a split-second before our minds can register it, so we're primed for fight or flight before we really know it. Evolution failed to phase out this reflex, so even in the absence of real threat, our hearts start beating fast, our faces flush, and we begin saying things we won't mean the next day, or even in the next hour. We call it *the heat of the moment.* You see it in cartoons: the boss man with steam geysering from his head, or the woman with exclamation points flying from her mouth like daggers.

Of the night

When Ray Charles sings it, you know salvation must be near. We have to drop deep into darkness before the morning comes. In the film of the same name, Sydney Poitier slaps a white man. He says: *They call me Mr. Tibbs.* It's 1967. Lots of things are on fire.

Packing

It's hard to know who is really "packing heat" and who is just posturing. The phrase seems to proliferate: music videos and video games, the songs they play in spin class, *Law & Order*, every action movie from *Die Hard* to *Mad Max: Fury Road.* Do women pack heat? Even when women carry guns, the phrase seems decidedly masculine. Then, a student of mine—a woman, older than I, a mother of three—confides she always carries a gun. "It's not something I advertise, but I do have a concealed weapons permit." I'm speechless. Perhaps my lip turns down, suggesting a question, a judgment of some kind. "Yeah," she says, "I just feel safer knowing I have what the bad guys have."

Pre-

I never follow recipes. Perhaps this is my small rebellion in a life otherwise spent heeding the rules. I mix cake batter and pour it into a Bundt pan, say, or I arrange winter vegetables on a roasting tray, but then I'm ready—ready to slip these encumbrances inside the oven and be done, wash my hands and wipe them on my pants since I have never invested in an apron. I'm ready to head back to my book or my desk with its papers fluttering like so many pairs of wings. Forget about preheating or setting the timer; I'm certain I'll smell the food when it's done.

Steam

It's a kind of heat, but it's also a kind of song—a show tune—which is the kind of song I like best. Before I ever saw *The Pajama Game* performed on stage or screen, I saw Georgette Franklin—sweet Georgette!—transform herself into a slinky, sexy diva and belt out this number on *Mary Tyler Moore.* Her boyfriend Ted is embarrassed. He doesn't want Georgette showing off her body that way—skimpy black leotard, transparent tights—or is it her talent that he wants her to hide? Carol Haney has a version of the song, as do Shirley MacLaine, Patti Page, Doris Day, Ella Fitzgerald, and Liza Minnelli. Every singer's version is different, but all of them begin with a visceral-sonic pop-hiss-fizz, an erotic onomatopoeia: *I've got ::cling cling:: fsssss steam heat.*

"The Heat" (Comedy)

It may be my favorite funny movie of all time. A serious, by-the-book FBI agent (Sandra Bullock) is forced to team up with a hot-headed, street-wise detective (Melissa McCarthy) in order to bring down the head of a treacherous Boston crime ring. It's a movie about female friendship that passes the Bechdel test with flying colors: two women who both have names and talk to each other (humorously and at length) about something (everything) besides a man. It's the reason we quip about anything overrated: "Is it served in Jesus's shoe?" It's the reason we shout about anything invasive: "Get fuck out my house!" And it's the reason I say lovingly to my spouse, "I'm going to bring you that sandwich," and she, looking me square in the face, replies, "Throw out that sandwich."

Wave

When I was four years old I got my tonsils out. No big deal, but when my parents brought me home, the city was in the midst of a heat wave. Temperatures soared to over a hundred degrees; we had no air-conditioning, so I sat sweating by the screen door. The nights were no better: the house gathered heat that radiated inward. I ate ice cream and whined *it's so hot.* I had a fever. I whimpered and slept fitfully, the covers kicked off. I kept hearing the words *heat wave*, and imagined the heat like a tsunami, the crest curling but never quite smashing down. The water just keeps building and building until it floods.

White

"Dare you see a Soul / *at the White Heat?*" Emily Dickinson asks. Heat loses all color at its uppermost limit, a heat so bright it blinds. It might be, if we squint hard enough, the light of heaven. Dickinson uses the forge as an analogy for creative and spiritual expansion; we must dare to lose ourselves, to become *hot*, to disappear into the light. We become malleable, melted, misshapen—in order to become something useful, enlightened, or beautiful. In blacksmithing, white heat represents the temperature "at which a body becomes brightly incandescent."

Workout

I've signed up for a workout program called "The Daily Burn." The commercials are so convincing, and I get to try it for 30 days free. So far, I've watched two workouts while sitting on the couch eating popcorn. The leader has a broad torso rippling with muscle, bald head gleaming (one could say he is *hot*, if one goes for that kind of thing). He exclaims, *Okay now, ladies, are we warmed up?* Then they get to work, skipping an imaginary jump rope, staggering in "the drunken ape." They all keep smiling, no matter how much it hurts.

Never

Yoga

I have bad memories of ballet class, and isn't yoga like dancing in a way, teaching the muscles how to lengthen, how to lean, how to turn elastic as rubber bands? All my springs are coiled tight for bouncing. My love even calls me Tigger sometimes. I watch her step out of the studio from my warm perch in the coffee shop across the street. Steam rises from her body. Steam rises from all the yogis' bodies in unison, in pseudo-cirrus reverie. They are shrouded. They are turning to clouds. They wrap scarves around their long, exposed necks, all of them, thin and elegant. They tuck their bony feet deep inside fleece-lined boots. I only have eyes for one of them, but I am watching all of them. Icicles dangle from the eaves, pointing down like arrows as if to say, *See here: these bodies have melted into their most fluid selves.*

I am solid. I hold a latte in my hand, which I have just ordered so it will be hot for her when she steps inside. The little bell above the door tinkles softly. Her cheeks are still burning from the heated room and the fire that yogis are taught to stoke inside them. I want to kiss her right here, right now, *always*, but she is not like that—not one for spectacle or display. She is always water flowing away from a scene. I am still land, of course, still solid, but I follow her everywhere with my eyes and with the secret compass lodged inside my throat. Eventually, I follow her to yoga class. She doesn't have to ask. People have crossed oceans for love, scaled mountains for love. *Why is a mat my mountain?* I notice, and then try not to notice, that when I hollow out my back in Cow and raise my chin, my clavicles still sink into my skin. No sharp crescent-moon rises out of the flesh. I notice, and then try not to notice, that when I lift myself into Wheel, there is nothing of the full circle about me. I only creak and cringe.

But there she is on her mat, doing beautiful things with her body. In a small way, we have scaled this mountain together. I feel so grateful and so vulnerable at once. *What to do now?* My sternum is full of suggestions, that hard ridge above my soft heart. *Stop anticipating. Stop analyzing. Just breathe.* She touches my hand in *Savasana*—only a light brush of her fingers, but it is enough. I lie supine and gaze at the stars.

Song

I have bad memories of singing. Not the earliest, not the baby song or the toddler song—nonsense burbling as echo from the womb. Nor even the kindergarten song—sitting crisscross applesauce on the worn carpet, pudgy hands clapping a beat, the wheels on the bus going 'round and 'round. But shortly after. When the world began to scowl. Hands clamped to ears. Sidelong smirk. So I shut up after that. Whispered and lip-synced whenever singing was required.

But here I am, somehow, in a roomful of women, on a summer Tuesday evening, making strange noises with my breath. We've trilled *Yoo Hoo!* to each other in British accents, and held our hands to our soft bellies while murmuring *yum*... None of it feels like singing, so we're able to let go and laugh—yet all of it is singing. It turns out singing begins in the body, becoming aware of the body as an instrument of sound.

And since the body is the instrument, we grow powerful and vulnerable at the same time. When your body is the instrument, any wrong note, any discord, feels as though you, yourself, are wrong. Singing is all about tuning your body, attuning to the slightest shift of posture: the lift of the ribs, the well of the pelvis, the slight rise of an eyebrow. You need to become liquid with song—not the ordinary solid cage of muscle and bone.

We're in a room with a piano, a small stage, and rickety chairs. It's the Bellingham Academy of Arts for Youth, and any minute now, children are going to stream in to rehearse *The Music Man.* I remember watching that movie with my parents and bouncing in my seat, leaning forward and aching to sing: *Till there was you…* vowels warbling up into the stratosphere. In a few months' time, I'll be performing with some of those children in a recital. The youngest will go first, singing the Tigger song, and then the eight-year-olds, and then me: so nervous in my cowboy boots and twirly skirt. But there will be no stopping it: I'll stand up to the microphone, and my teacher will sit at the piano, smiling her encouraging smile. I'll launch into it, diving, as my teacher says, into the song that already exists in the air. *Oh, give me a home…* And then the lesser-known verse: *Oh give me a land, with its white diamond sand, and the light from the glittering stream / where glideth along, the snowy white swan, like a maid in her heavenly dream…* And though I know my pitch is in flux, every round "o" floats from me like a bubble (so many songs, it turns out, rely on that long "o" sound, a vowel that opens the back of the throat so music can rush in). Then the audience will join me on the chorus, raucous and alive: *and never is heard, a discouraging word, and the sky is not cloudy all day…*

But for now I'm just humming, deep in my belly, feeling the way the core muscles support every sound. I'm holding my hands at the side of my ribs to feel the way they can expand, and stay expanded, on their own. I feel the stickiness of my lungs as they adhere to the ribs in order to hold more breath. I'm standing on one foot—wobbly, unbalanced, laughing—to ignite the muscles of song.

Failure

"No environment could be better for young women who have feared it all their lives," Sister Ann Cornelia says as she writes *Failure* with a flourish on the board. Here I am, somehow, in a roomful of others like me: all of us soon-to-be freshmen, soon-to-be fourteen, future valedictorians and National Merit Scholars. Or so we've been told. All of us promised since infancy that we were fit to be Ivy League.

"Most of you have never been pushed to your fullest potential." She faces us now, chalky hands pressed against her middle button firmly. She is small and round and sure of herself. Her clothes are dark with white smudges like a winter sky. "But the day will come when your best won't be good enough. You will fail at something here, *for once*—I promise you that—and you will be better for it, forever."

Not me, though. I am not allowed to fail. I gather other people's expectations like daisies in a field. I weave them into plain but respectable garlands. At Holy Names Academy, my first year, there are only flowers, and I keep collecting them, the way I have learned to do—not stopping to smell them anymore, only bending to pluck, then tuck them in my temperate bouquet: *A after A after A.* But the next year, there is chemistry. The next year there are numbers doing things I don't quite understand. There is also Bridget who shares the lab desk with me: Bridget who writes poems on graph paper, Bridget who braids her own hair, Bridget who wants to go to alternative school in British Columbia.

I have chemistry with Bridget. Any way you say it, the statement is true. We start tie-dyeing shirts together. We start writing and casting a play. Soon, I am borrowing hats with crushed velvet flowers that flop carelessly over my eyes. I forget I am a Virgo and pledge my devotion to a less exacting sign.

When it arrives, the F appears almost neutral, like a fingerprint that hasn't been scanned yet—just a lone blue letter centered at the top of a page. It is both unexpected and entirely deserved. I cannot argue with it, this F I have earned through relentless inattention, and yet I have to lean against the wall to keep from tipping over. My legs are wobbly now, my joints unhinged.

"So what?" Bridget says. "It's just a letter. Let's tear up our tests and make streamers!" But alas, I am not the kind of girl who can part ways so quickly and completely with convention.

My lungs are sticky as I try to steady my breath, as I lean over and somberly whisper: "I don't think we should see so much of each other anymore."

Success

It's ridiculous, really: a PhD, a "Doctor of Philosophy." In my family, doctors (*real* doctors) are revered; we submit to their authority and do anything they say. And of course, the unspoken Jewish expectation: *you'll meet a nice boy, a doctor maybe, why not?* It's expected of young girls, young women. Sure, you can go to college, but don't make a habit of it.

I've met nice boys, but they're not doctors or lawyers or shrewd businessmen. They are novelists, poets, teachers, carpenters. None of them are Jewish. Their beliefs fluctuate from day to day. We drink lots of coffee and take long walks. We hold hands. We walk along rivers and mountains and lakes. We walk to funky cinemas with disco balls rotating in the ceiling, making everything sparkle.

Philosophy, in Greek, means "love of wisdom." So, I suppose I'm about to become a "doctor of wisdom," or a "doctor of love." But I'm neither of these things. I've stumbled into graduate school in complete ignorance, as if I've been sleepwalking, inching slowly backward down a dark alley. It's only now, minutes before my oral exams, that I've begun to wake up, take my bearings, turn on the lights. *How did I get here? Where am I?*

I'm sitting in a windowless classroom, waiting for my professors. I've brought a bouquet of irises and tulips; I've brought pastries from the groovy shop downtown. Are these bribes? Perhaps. I've dressed like an adult, in a nice skirt and shoes with a heel. I've even put on lipstick. But my fingernails are bitten down, and there's a big pimple on my chin. The seams in me always show.

I've been studying, spending long hours in the library with Montaigne and Hazlitt and Lamb. I know Didion and E.B. White as if they're old friends. I've made flash cards. I've memorized quotes. I've constructed arguments about representations of the self on the page. But success seems unfathomable, unthinkable, for a girl who's never had any idea where she's going. At this moment, I feel blank as a new notebook. Nothing has been inscribed.

Manicure

I had dressed like an adult since I was a child, a miniature version of my mother. At eleven, she gave me a tube of lipstick just her shade, rouge, mascara, and powder. She said people might mistake us for sisters and smiled at the thought. By the time I was twenty-one, I was weary from a decade of make-up and polish—the way my mother insisted we must *make up* for something, the fact we were not "natural beauties."

No more high heels, I vowed. For another decade at least, not even a dress, not once. I cut up my stockings. I kept my hair short and my face bare. Perhaps others assumed I was marking myself and my love affair with a woman. Perhaps they even inferred that I was "the man" in our relationship. Evidence: hadn't I also purchased a Pierre Cardin tie, a blush-worthy impulse buy? But I think it was adolescent rebellion at last, years overdue—this stalwart refusal to gussy.

The day before our wedding, also years overdue, my beloved suggests we get a manicure. Our best friend is with us. She knows a place. "It might be fun," she laughs, "to do something girly together for once."

Now the most important women in my life are sitting side by side, having their nails done, chatting softly and choosing a color. They are lesbians. They are feminists. They are not worried about the implications of a little gloss and tint on their hands. *So why am I?* "This your first time in nail salon?" the man at the counter asks. I nod, sheepishly, but still I linger near the door, resisting the chairs and magazines. The seams in me always show.

"Your turn, miss," a young woman beckons. Her face is an open door. This is my chance to be *normal*, to be *one of the girls*, to participate in the rituals of femininity that have so long eluded me. This time, I can even do so on my own terms.

I place my hands in hers, gingerly, the way I will place my hands in my beloved's tomorrow, when we stand before the small crowd to exchange our vows. "Your nails are very short," she observes, a diplomatic alternative to *ragged* or *gnawed.* "I will soak your hands first, then push down your cuticles so we can see the moons. Yes?"

All at once, years of longing and fear and other feelings I don't quite recognize are streaming from my eyes. I blot them quickly before we begin. "You are all right, miss?" I want to say how my mother isn't coming to my wedding, how my mother doesn't believe in my love. And I want to say how sad I am to be so relieved that she won't have a chance to ruin everything. But instead, I nod my head, less sheepish this time: "Yes, please, I want to see the moons."

Highlights

I lean my head into her hands and instinctively nuzzle them, like a cat. My eyes close and I hum quietly—a resonant *yum*—while she massages my scalp with lavender oil. These days, I get touched like this only by professionals: my hairdresser, my massage therapist, my chiropractor. My skin tingles at their touch. I feel a quick flush of shame at my pleasure.

She lifts one lock of hair, then another. I feel the gentle tug on my scalp, but even when I open my eyes I can't see what she's doing; without my glasses I'm a blur in the mirror, a faint outline of head and shoulders draped with a black cloth. I know she's pondering what to do with me today. My hair is at the in-between stage where nothing seems quite right.

How about highlights? she muses, almost to herself. Highlights? My hair has always been what I call "chestnut": brown but with an undertone of red. At certain angles, it's had a sheen to it, though my bangs get frizzy or oily, depending on the day. Most often they hang in one lanky bunch above my eyebrows. I've managed to arrive into my fifties without dyeing my hair, the gray strands barely noticeable until they spring up like coarse wire. I've never wanted to get caught in the hair-dyeing cycle, roots showing like flags of age that must be quickly hidden.

But lately, the gray hairs have been accumulating—quietly, like radicals gathering for subversion—and so I now see wide swathes of them when I brush my hair or push my bangs back with a headband. I see them, but I don't see them, averting my eyes. It's not a stylish wing of gray, like Susan Sontag, or a silver sheen like Helen Mirren. My gray is unruly, dowdy, stripping my hair of whatever vital spark it once possessed.

We'll do it subtly, very natural, she says, gazing at me in the mirror. I can't see her eyes, but she's smiling. Her hands cup my shoulders, firm but gentle, as if she's about to steer me the right direction on a trail. *Yes?*

How can I resist her, this woman who has examined every inch of my head? This woman who washes my hair and smooths it against my scalp, who is always happy to see me, who wants only to make me lovely? We've talked about everything and nothing. But if I say *yes*—if I agree to be highlighted—will I still be myself? Will the highlights announce themselves, tell the world I no longer trust my own body to act in its best interests?

She's waiting for my answer. The phone rings, and I hear the snip of other scissors, the roar of the blow dryer. The sound system is playing "Hallelujah," a song I've been hearing lately everywhere. This song always makes me both sad and happy at the same time; it's a prayer of longing and not-quite-forgiveness. It's a voice that wants to shout in jubilation to the heavens—you can it hear it straining to find its pitch—but finds itself hobbled by the failings of an earthbound body.

It's a song I've been singing my whole life.

Without speaking, I say *yes*. I nod, and she claps her hands, hurries off to get the foils and dyes. My blurred self and I wait quietly for her return. I know she'll gently lift each hank of hair, carefully paint each strand until it shines.

Infidelity

Follow your heart! the poets exhort. I shrug my shoulders: *What else would I follow?* These are the lyrics I've been singing my whole life: songs of love and longing, passion and devotion. If I am anything, I am loyal. My eyes never wander. My feet are invariably warm.

But in college, when I begin to listen to radical folk singers like Ani DiFranco, I'm surprised, then riveted by the song called "Shameless," and I play it hour after hour, the repeat button set on my small dorm stereo. What I can't get over is how candid the speaker is about wanting another man's wife; this is the first time I have ever heard a woman express such unabashed desire for another. I flush every time DiFranco's voice dips low, slices through study time with a guttural moan. If my roommate walks in, I plunge for the pause button. I consider investing in a pair of headphones.

Little do I know that in just a few years I will find myself promised to a man. I will say *Yes, OK*, to marrying him, *No, I'd rather not* to the suggestion of a ring. He laughs at me. "You're never about the bling, are you?" But he knows he can trust me, even with my bare left hand. He knows I'm not one for shirking my commitments. I always call, even if I'm only running a few minutes behind.

So I will not be able to *name this*. I will not be able to *explain this*. When I finally pick up the phone, days too late, I will wince at his fury, though I will know it is what I deserve. *Shameless*, he says, *a snake in the grass*. Later, in a letter: *Men don't choose a woman like you because you're the hottest. They choose a woman like you because you're the safest.*

Why I didn't call him first, why I didn't sever one cord before I tied another—I couldn't say. I was raised with Captain Von Trapp telling Baronness Schraeder on the Austrian terrace, *You can't marry someone when you're in love with someone else.* This he does before he kisses Fräulein Maria in the gazebo by the water, before they sing together about having done *something good.*

My heart, strange Geiger counter, is sending signals only my body can read. Perhaps the gazebo is the room without a door. Surely it is the glass house from which I must never throw stones. I am alone with the woman

I love by a lake in darkness. It is spring, and our bodies are acting at last in their own best interests. My place. Her place. It hardly matters where we go next. *I can't even slow this down, let alone stop this.* The night is a stringed instrument. The future an encore. *We cannot top this*, even if we try.

Fidelity

The root word of fidelity means *faith.* As in devotion or belief. An infidel is one who has lost her belief. And, as with any faith, doubt comes into play. *Doubt*, the philosopher Paul Tillich stressed, *isn't the opposite of faith; it is an element of faith.* Or, to put it more lyrically, from Sylvia Plath: *I talk to God but the sky is empty.*

Fidelity also means accuracy, exactitude. As in *fidelity to the facts.* Or it means the quality of sound: *high fidelity,* as in a record or a film—each note clear and true. So many meanings for one word that, on the face of it, seems so simple and steadfast.

When I think of fidelity I think of my dog. Though her name is not "Fido" (a name that must, I hope, have the same origin), she keeps me always in her sights. She arranges herself in ways that seem meant to guard me from whatever, or whoever, might take me unaware (at the moment, for example, she has curled up behind my chair, blocking the doorway). She often has her eyes closed, but her ears twitch and she can be on her feet in a flash. She's a small dog—only twenty pounds, with a foxlike face and a white plume for a tail—but her bark is that of a Great Dane's.

She will bark at mailmen and anyone who delivers a package to my door. She will bark at the jingle of another dog's collar in the street. She will bark at things invisible to my eye and ear, anything that might be a threat. She will bark to alert me, too, of friends arriving, wagging her tail so vigorously it's a blur. Her pant becomes a smile, says: *look who's here!*

She's been my dog for almost ten years now, though I dreamed of her long before plucking her from the listings on Petfinder. She came to me as a puppy—all legs and nose and eyes—and I often felt at a loss, consulting my *Puppies for Dummies* book constantly, memorizing the steps for potty training, leash training, socialization, hygiene. She poked her head out of the cat carrier I'd used to pick her up, tongue lolling, eyes rolling from side to side. I could hardly speak, sure that anything I did might cause irrevocable harm. I touch her flank while we sleep, feeling her slow steady breath. I kiss her snout when we wake, nuzzle her under the chin. We make a full circle.

I once thought I'd have a daughter, a baby I could sing to sleep. I once thought I'd have a husband who would hold this baby lightly in the crook of his arm. I once thought my home would be filled with voices at all hours, a family working together at the mundane tasks—dishes, homework, puzzles—that make up a life. I believed these were facts, and anything else a poor imitation, inaccurate.

But, as it turns out, it's just me and my dog. We are faithful to one another, and to this house that does not seem to mind its sparse occupancy. My dog roams the backyard, ears alert for any intruder; she comes inside and watches my every move. I stretch into Downward Dog, Crocodile, Cat and Cow under her scrutiny. I sing to her the songs I'm learning, and she listens, sighing, stretching to make herself long as pulled taffy. Our sky is not empty, oh no. The night is a duet; it teems with a thousand stars.

Cars

This is how I thought it would be the morning of my sixteenth birthday: peering through the pink lace curtains to discover a new car on the drive, a thick pink ribbon draped over the dome like a headband, knotted and looped in a giant bow. Not a convertible, mind you—impractical given all the Seattle mist and fog—but something even less practical: a vintage yellow Volkswagen bug. So what if it had a manual transmission? I could learn. (It turns out I couldn't.) So what if parts were expensive and hard to come by? I could befriend a mechanic, or better still, learn the ins and outs of the retro vehicle repair world. (It turns out I couldn't.) But the fact is, I woke up at sixteen, and my mother drove me to piano lessons before school like always. My father picked me up after school, just the same. No one said a word about my driver's license, and it was another three years before I held it in the palm of my hot little hand.

I blame television and the years I spent with my nose pressed against the screen. Here's another: I thought I would lose my virginity in a red Mustang with white leather interiors and an ample back seat. It gets worse. I thought the boy who would own this car, who would wash it every Sunday like it was his religion, buffing the hood with turtle wax, keeping the white wall tires clean and bright as fresh-fallen snow—the boy who would love me the way I loved literature—would sprinkle red rose petals over those white leather seats and read me a poem he had written before we undressed without any difficulty and made love with the flexibility of gymnasts, the confidence of characters in the novel I was writing at the time. Worse still: all this would happen at a drive-in theater where they were showing *The Rocky Horror Picture Show.* I have since seen the movie, and my virginity is long gone, but I have never been to a drive-in or had much of any kind of sex in a car.

Then, this: I thought I would get married someday—possibly to the boy with the red Mustang, because I'm romantic like that. I imagined we would each drive separately to the ceremony, I in my vintage yellow Volkswagen bug wearing a short white dress that still got stuck in the door. We'd meet in a garden or a public park, say our vows, exchange our rings in relative solitude. Then, he'd lead me over to the powder-blue convertible he'd hidden in the brush—yes, a convertible this time!—and we'd drive down the Oregon Coast eating Triscuits and oysters straight from the tin. Instead, I married a woman in a restaurant called the Black Cat where once, years before, we ordered dessert and looked deeply into each other's eyes and realized we were in it for the long haul. We drove a rental to the wedding first and the hotel after, and I was so happy and relieved and exhausted that I couldn't tell you what make or model it was.

•—•

I learned to drive stick shift in a yellow VW bug. It's true. Somehow, between my junior and senior years of college, I found myself high-tailing it to Wyoming with five of my best male buddies, where we would live together in a tiny house while the boys worked the oil fields. My friend Don picked me up at my parents' house in the San Fernando Valley in his yellow VW bug; I like to imagine he cheerfully tooted the horn as he came up the driveway, but probably not. I do remember my father leaning in the driver's side window and handing Don a screwdriver: a talisman, I suppose, to protect his daughter on the journey.

It astounds me, even now, the things my parents let me do: backpack through Europe at 17; go away to college at Berkeley; come home after my nervous breakdown. I'd spent that spring recovering in my childhood bedroom. I attended community college with my friend A.J., where we got stoned and went to Philosophy of the Occult 101. We read Carlos Castaneda together and sat in camaraderie in the Mulholland hills, not saying much.

And now my mom and dad waved goodbye as Don and I backed out of the driveway in his yellow VW bug. He would teach me the mechanics of manual shifting in various parking lots along the road from California to Casper. Of course there was much grinding of the gears, and many instances of the car jolting to a stall, but Don was patient and good-humored, and eventually I got it: the smooth lift of the clutch, the coordination of the gearshift, finding the sweet spot where the two interjoin.

When we got to Wyoming, the rest of the boys had already found us a house and had rigged up various sleeping arrangements in the basement. I got one of the bedrooms, being the only girl, and Don got the other, being the fussy one. My friends went off to work in the oil fields early each day, and I found work at the only place I could: a fast-food pizza joint where I spent my days rolling out the pre-made dough, splattering it with canned sauce and pre-grated cheese. I bought myself a used Vespa scooter to commute into town, and I toodled along the quiet roads, the vast Wyoming sky above me, my grease-stained shoes just inches from the ground. The one perk was free pizza, and I brought home boxes and boxes for the ravenous boys to eat.

What was I really doing there? The townspeople, it turned out (I heard the gossip from a coworker), thought we were living in some kind of orgy house and that I was a woman of "loose morals." While it was true that I had, at one time or another, slept with a few of those boys, I had never done so at the same time and considered myself rather old-fashioned: a believer in love. My current boyfriend, Pat, occupied my bed, and we took trips in his van to campsites around the state. He was a nomad: saving money for a sailing trip around the world, so our affair was necessarily transient. After that summer, I would be on my way to northern California to resume college. The boys would scatter to their various futures. We lived in a space of interlude.

One night in August, after making love with Pat, I felt a sharp twinge in my pelvis; it passed quickly, but I knew something was up, and four weeks later I would be in the hospital in Eureka, California, having a fallopian miscarriage. The pain of an embryo caught in that narrow place is not something that can adequately be described. Pat came to visit—a port of call—and we showered together and cried, but none of it felt real, as if everything were happening through a frosted window and I couldn't wedge it open enough to let in clear light.

I thought I always wanted, eventually, to own a convertible: to have the ability to transform a vehicle from enclosed to open, to be seen as you cruise down the street. But every time I've ridden in a topless car, the experience hasn't been pleasant: sun in your eyes, hair windblown and tangling, windburn on your cheeks. No—now I want a car solid and quiet and fully contained, purring along the highway with nary a ripple. I want music to fill that car, and the windows tinted. I want airbags on every side for protection.

•—•

My friend Ben, who was sometimes my boyfriend, had borrowed the car from a friend who had borrowed it from his father to drive to college in the Pacific Northwest. It was a Buick, or possibly a Chevrolet. I think I would have recognized a Ford. Ben may have had to pay him something or just promise to refill the tank when we were done. I was only newly licensed then and nervous that I'd have to take the wheel in a crisis. More than once I asked, tugging on my crushed velvet dress, squatting in my too-tall shoes, "Does somebody—anybody—connected with this car have Triple A?"

I remember the date: December 10, 1998. I probably still have a ticket stub somewhere, since Ben was driving me to Jazz Alley in Seattle. I had never heard live jazz before. I didn't know who Gene Harris was or what it meant when he stepped onto the stage in that candlelit room, the hands around me crackling like hot kernels, popping to unexpected life.

I did know that I loved Ben, or I thought I did. But earlier that week in sociology class, the professor had said we could write down anonymously—and this was key—any question we had about nature or behavior or the so-called "human experience." He was really earning his paycheck, it seemed to me, since our questions were impossibly hard. I wrote, trying to disguise my bubbly script with a blurry, almost pixelated print: *Can you be in love with someone's mind but not their body?* People said different things. Most of the girls said *yes*, you could, and you were more likely to grow to love the body in question if you already loved the mind. Most of the boys said *no*, though, or *iffy*, because physical attraction came first, and real love, if it happened at all, came later: an affinity of body and mind. The professor said he honestly wasn't sure how to respond, which I took as an ominous sign.

I loved Ben, but I was having trouble with the physical part of desire. I had my theories as to why. He was shorter and smaller than I. His Adam's apple troubled me, the way it protruded from his throat. I thought I might love him better in an ascot. But that night he was wearing a tie with a piano keyboard on it and a gray blazer that seemed, even surreptitiously, to bulk him up. He looked handsome to me, and the cap he wore increased his height. We returned to campus just before midnight, then sat in the car to watch the numbers change.

"I love that moment when it's suddenly the next day," I told him. He held my hand, and we watched the green digits on the dashboard turn. We sat like lovers on a beach at sunrise—so rapt and breathless, our anticipation shrinking us to tiny silhouettes.

But then it started raining, and this was a lower campus parking lot. We both lived about a mile away in one of the upper dorms. With silent gallantry, Ben opened the door to the backseat, and I climbed inside without asking questions. It was a bench with soft upholstery, not much room but that was all right. What happened was this: we kissed for hours. There was no expectation and really no possibility of doing anything more than kissing—because our school was Christian and we had been told in various ways how disappointed Umpire Jesus would be if we turned that dangerous corner toward third base (even second was iffy); because sex on campus was an infraction that could earn us a demerit (think of our clean records, our good grades!); and because we were afraid of sex even more than we were afraid of demerits (an already sizeable fear). So we just kept kissing, and the rain just kept beating down on the windows, blurring the street lights, softening their glow.

I don't know if I could ever kiss that long again without wanting something more, without taking something off, without feeling that I needed what came next. But in the early hours of December 11, 1998, there was no next. There was only the eternal back seat of that Buick, that possibly Chevrolet, and I think this is what they mean by *swooning*—the way I seemed to levitate out of my own skin, the way I had never felt more alive in my whole life, the way I thought *I could get an A+ in kissing now if they gave grades for that*, which was satisfying because there was so much in my life I sensed I might not be able to master.

When the green digits blinked 3:18, we realized the rain had stopped, so we stopped, too. We buttoned our coats, and we smoothed our hair, and we walked hand in hand toward the upper dorms under a drippy brown canopy of leaves. The feeling between us was fading already. I knew that it wouldn't come back.

But sometimes when I'd see that dented American car idling around campus, my breath would catch in my throat, and I'd remember what was possible—that my body could get warm like that, could make its own heat, even in December in the Pacific Northwest, even after hours in a backseat with the engine turned off. In other words, my mind wasn't the only part of me with a driving force.

•—•

The force that through the green fuse drives the flower / Drives my green age… Dylan Thomas wrote those lines in 1933, when he was just nineteen years old. Those are, possibly, the most famous words he penned—an evocation of exuberant youth—but most of us forget what comes next: ... *that blasts the roots of trees / Is my destroyer.* Thomas knew the same force spurs both life and death, love and the end of love.

When I was sixteen years old, my Jewish youth group put on Dylan Thomas's radio play *Under Milk Wood.* It's an odd choice for a bunch of teenage thespians: full of Welsh idiom and dead characters moving about in dreams. But we had the kind of counselors who acted like lit fuses: wildly enthusiastic about any activity, with hair that seemed electrocuted. They actually couldn't have been much older than we were—20 or 21—hired to keep a bunch of marginally Jewish teens occupied for a few hours a day.

We met in a home called *Chai* House: *Chai* means "life" in Hebrew, and is also the number eighteen, symbolizing luck. Many of us girls wore *chai* ornaments around our necks or wrists, given to us by our parents as charms. Even so, the "Jewish" part of the Jewish youth group really didn't interest us much. We just wanted to huddle together on the ratty couches in that house and smoke cigarettes in the backyard. We wanted to tuck our legs under us and speak a coded language only we could understand.

This would have been the summer of 1975. Our counselors wore striped cotton tunics with kangaroo pockets and went barefoot. Their bodies were lean and angular and moved fast. They always looked like they had just rolled out of bed (perhaps after a night of intense sex), ready for whatever the day might bring, and they smelled of garlic and incense. We were all a little in love with them, so when they brought copies of *Under Milk Wood* into the house, flinging them to us like Frisbees, we had no choice but to go along.

We each played multiple roles. I was by turns Rosie Probert, the dead lover of the narrator, Captain Cat; Mae Rose Cottage, seventeen-year-old virgin who drew circles around her nipples with lipstick; and Polly Garter, a young wife who wanted scores of babies. I highlighted all my lines and practiced, but the counselors were demanding directors, pushing us to really get inside these characters' heads. *What motivates her?* a counselor would ask, earnestly, his face close to mine. *What does she really want?* I had no answers to these questions, but I responded by speaking my lines louder, with the same inflections. We really had no idea what we were saying, but we gamely shouted the dialogue at one another, cracking up for no reason at all.

I'd lost my virginity the year before (well, not really *lost*, I knew exactly where it was) to a boy in the youth group: not in a vehicle, but in my childhood bedroom. Before that, though, my young paramour and I had often made out in his car, a blue Ford that chugged into empty parking lots on the sly. I still remember that feeling you get when the car stops, and the boy turns the engine off. The crank of the emergency brake, so loud in the sudden quiet. The dark pressing in on the windows; the engine pinging as it cools. The knowledge that you could stop now, say you want to go home. Knowing the moment lasts only an instant. Once you get started, another force takes over: one that wants all of you to melt.

That boy began to ignore me once we had "done it," and he had another girlfriend anyway: a girl with long blond hair, one of those Jewish girls who could easily pass for a goy. We still saw each other nearly every day at the *Chai* house, and I'd watch him as he performed his parts. He gestured broadly and overdid the accent. He had the barest hint of a mustache on his long, thin face which gave him the air of a scruffy con man. Someone you could never trust.

One day, the counselor got a little carried away in his quest for stellar performances. He sat next to me on the couch, smoking a cigarette, and asked what it would take for me to really *feel* the part of Mae and her longing for love. He said: *you have to call up a memory of pain and use it!* I kept my gaze on my lap, and maybe I giggled, because he took his cigarette and brought it close to my arm, to the innermost curve of the elbow. *I'm just going to touch you lightly, so the pain can be a physical memory.* All the other kids now circled around us, including my boy. I didn't look up. Everyone grew absurdly quiet, breaths held. I didn't tell the counselor I already had enough pain on which to draw. I just waited to see what would happen next.

I can't remember if we actually ended up giving a performance of *Under Milk Wood.* It's a radio play and so isn't meant to be watched—rather only heard, the audience calling up their own visions of these characters as they sleepwalk through their dreams. I recall various microphones and *test, test, test,* so we probably did at least one full run-through, our voices tinny and canned on tape, capturing nothing of that *Chai* House and its well-worn furniture, the scuffle of adolescents trying hard to enact all their roles. Dylan Thomas himself acted in *Under Milk Wood* just a year before his death at age 39. He died of pneumonia, though he had been well on his way to drinking himself into a coma.

The force that drives the water through the rocks / Drives my red blood; that dries the mouthing streams / turns mine to wax. I wonder: how do we keep a steady course through the contradictory forces that guide us?

•—•

Most days I feel like I'm standing on a see-saw at the edge of the ocean, one foot straddling each side—courage and cowardice, ease and awkwardness. I feel a wind whipping up in the distance, but I sure like the look of those waves.

What I know is that joy comes easily to me, and so does driving. Not stick shift, of course, but that's another story. My father used to say that he admired my zeal, that I had a tremendous "zest for life." I think he was right, but it was also like the song from Bible School warned—I had learned to hide my light under a bushel. Since I could never picture a bushel exactly, I pictured this instead: my light a candle in a votive cup, pretty but breakable, perched on that see-saw in the threatening wind as waves crested the rocks around it.

My mother once said, "You have a voice for radio. My concern is that you have a face for radio, too." Her words were a see-saw. I tried to lean forward and focus on the compliment. Years later, I drove out in a borrowed car on a blustery day to do a radio show in eastern Kentucky. On the highway, water froze between the rocks, icicles suspended like fallen chandeliers. This landscape looked as fierce and fragile as I had ever seen from the front seat of the gray Volkswagen golf—a Volkswagen at last!—and I felt the way I think you're supposed to feel in cars: happy and safe but also wild and free. See? Saw.

I do most of my mulling and a good bit of my writing behind the wheel. I talk into the open space. I jot at stoplights. The daughter and granddaughter of traveling salesmen, my heart quickens at the sight of interstate on-ramps and winding country roads. I am attracted to long distances, the means before the end, process and progression, everything arranged into segments. It seems most honest to say that I am in love with momentum.

Years ago, I was in love with my college roommate, too, though I didn't realize it then. Becky took me around her family's North Tacoma neighborhood in an old, sputtering car with a standard transmission, eager to help me learn. I got so flustered that I couldn't catch my breath. *It's the balancing of two feet instead of one*, I said. *I'm not good at shifting*, I said. Becky smiled at me, patted my shoulder, promised we'd try again another time. She had blond hair and blue eyes and pink cheeks, her face open as an envelope, impossibly kind. *Cinderella with a stick shift*, I thought to myself, then tried and tried to pry her image from my mind.

Junior year I befriended a different kind of girl. She wore hippie kerchiefs in her dark curls, slung a guitar over her lovely, fleshy shoulder. Sadness floated in the air around her, seeped into her soft, acoustic songs. For Summer, I could stay awake all night. I could pretend I wasn't concerned with schoolwork or stamps of approval from adult authority figures. She drove a maroon Honda Civic with a stick shift. She had a tape deck that played the Indigo Girls. When she passed me the cigarette she had pressed to her lips, I smoked it. What did I care for my little pink lungs? This was the closest I was going to get to a kiss.

T.S. Eliot wrote, *The end of all our exploring will / be to arrive where we started and / know the place for the first time.* He also wrote, *All is always now.* One night I found myself creeping into the same parking lot where Ben and I once kissed for hours. "I'll teach you to drive stick," Summer offered. "No one's around. We'll have fun." She held the door silently, and I climbed into the driver's seat. She placed her hand on my hand, and around we went, hour after hour, a carousel of terrible, jerking motions.

"Just relax," she said. "Try to feel it with your body, not master it with your mind." When I saw sunlight cresting spruces in the distance, I put my face down on the steering wheel and cried.

In the eternal recording studio, the interviewer leans in close to her microphone and says, "You're more jubilant in real life than I would have ever imagined, reading your work. Why do you suppose that is?" How do I tell her that sadness is always there, for everyone? It's either scrawled on the ragtop for all to see, or it's tucked under the hood—a subtle pain, a distant rattle.

•—•

A boyfriend once asked me, out of nowhere: *How many children do you want to have?*

It was a weird question, not really apropos of anything we'd been discussing. We sat at his tiny table in an alcove of his attic apartment; we both loved that apartment, though it grew quite hot in the Missoula summers. He lived above his landlord, an accountant who hunted in his spare time, and sometimes, in the fall, there'd be twelve antelope strung up in his garage. The landlord once invited us to a tasting party: before you can grind antelope into sausage, you need to grill up a sample medallion from each one—always one animal is tainted with fear's residue. It can ruin the whole batch.

This boy and I got along best on road trips. He had a tan Honda Civic, and once he even got to be on the radio show *Car Talk*, joking with Click and Clack as he asked them why he got shocked every time he touched the driver's side door. I remember how nervous he was as he waited on the line for his turn, his knee shaking. His voice—when we heard it later on broadcast—sounded so distant, but so happy. Click and Clack asked him if he wore synthetic fibers, and he replied, *Nope, only 100% cotton*, and they laughed, said they could tell Keith was a *100% cotton kind of guy*, which was true. When Keith told them the rear defroster didn't work they said: *You know what rear defrosters are good for on this car? Keeping your hands warm while you push it!* And they laughed and laughed, their voices so good-natured and jolly as they teased.

Keith and I took trips all over Montana and once broke down in the tiny town of Glacier on the east side of Glacier National Park. The only shop in town—a greasy, oil-stained garage, with two mechanics named Ace and Chance—said we'd need to wait at least two days for the parts. So we holed up in a roadside motel across the street and watched TV on the three available channels. We took walks that gave us views of the high mountains we still needed to cross.

We drove south to hot springs and east to a ghost town. Always, my bare feet ended up on the dash, my toes tapping to the rhythm of whatever soundtrack we chose. The case of cassette tapes and CDs lay on the floor of the passenger seat, and it was my job to rummage through them and determine the tone of the next hour or so. Our favorite was the jazz duo *Everything But the Girl*. The voice of the lead singer—a low and sultry alto—wove through the twangs of guitar and ripples of keyboard, their song "Driving" a perfect soundtrack, scenery rushing by in flashes. I reached over and laid my palm on Keith's knuckles, and he turned his hand over to intertwine his fingers with mine.

Once, when Keith and I had broken up (we were always breaking up, like ice on a river each spring), I played "Driving" over and over in my own car. I sang along, my voice terrible but somehow emboldened in the closed space. I drove around town looking, I admit it now, for Keith's car: in front of the gym, at the grocery store, parked at his apartment. I wasn't exactly stalking him (or maybe I was); I just wanted to know where he might be: to imagine him at the gym doing his reps, or at the grocery store buying bananas, or in his bed reading (I hoped he was alone, just reading). His car, an innocent bystander, waiting.

I've always loved how the word *question* stems from the root *quest*, as if each question leads you on a road trip—sometimes long, endless, sometimes short and sweet. I didn't know if, when Keith asked that question about children, he meant with him or by myself. I didn't know if I wanted children, let alone how many. So many nuances—I could only stand up and pace the few steps to his bed and lie down while the Missoula sun started to set. Below us there may have been antelope, with a memory of their elegant travels across the plains still alive in their quiet flesh.

Even today, I listen to *Car Talk*, though one of the brothers has Alzheimer's and can no longer do the show. Yet, somehow, their two voices emanate from the radio as they perform the puzzler, or recall previous shows with "stump the chump." Always, for the briefest of moments, I think of Keith when the theme music starts and those familiar voices speak to me from beyond. They welcome all callers with *Hello, you're on Car Talk*, and ask, with genuine interest, *What is your question?*

•—•

Always, some version of *How did I end up here?* Always, the Kierkegaardian imperative: that life is lived forward but understood, if at all, in reverse.

Consider: I have just turned twenty-two. The sky is empty of planes and clouds. September 11th is a fresh rift in the American landscape—not an anniversary yet, not something we have learned to memorialize.

I am about to start graduate school. The night before I drive to Bellingham, I sleep with my boyfriend in a marginal motel attached to an IHOP where I plan to involve myself with a stack of flapjacks and a variety of syrups just as soon as the sun comes up. I am hungry and curious to try everything, and these feelings extend far beyond food.

Charlie, my boyfriend, who is soon to become my fiancé, would have driven me to my new apartment three hours north if it weren't for the fact that his own car had been totaled in a recent accident. I don't own a car and have gotten by with rides from friends and bus service between the university transit center and my job selling shoes with Charlie at the mall. In fact, after I take out this stack of flapjacks, I'm going to kiss him goodbye and hop on a bus to Seattle where my parents will pick me up and lecture me about staying in the right lane and never exceeding the speed limit when I take solo command of their dark blue Honda Accord. They will follow in a U-Haul.

Charlie never replaces his car, which seems strange to me, but I suspect he doesn't have much money, and neither do I, so we never talk about it. Instead, he takes the train from Tacoma to Bellingham to visit me several times during my first year in grad school. In November, I walk to the Amtrak station in Fairhaven to meet him and we are so lovey at first, holding hands, snaking our arms around each other, until he stops, winded, on one of the many hills: "Just how far away from here do you live?"

I shrug. "I don't know. A couple of miles. Why?"

His bag is suddenly too heavy on his shoulder, but when I offer to take a turn carrying it, he snaps at me: "Now how would that look?" *Oh, I see. Because I'm the woman, and he's the man.* We are both irritated by this point and trudge on in silence, parallel shadows in the lean, autumn light.

I don't know why he asks me to marry him at the end of this trip, but I suspect it has to do with keeping our connection alive, giving us something to look forward to—to plan together. I say yes because I am having trouble concentrating. My mind wanders all the time but alights, invariably, on a woman in my introductory theory class. I am seeing a doctor, too, who has only recently confirmed that my body is experiencing a "thyroid malfunction." I have tumors growing in my throat—benign, but aggressive nonetheless. So when I wake up dreaming of Angie, my body dunk-tank drenched, I can dismiss this, too, as an "endocrine issue."

The next time Charlie visits, he asks me to pick him up in a car. "Take a cab if you have to," he says. "I'll pay. But I don't want to walk all that way again."

Angie, who I walk with most days after class, presses her keys into my slick, warm palm. "Take my car," she says. "It's Valentine's Day. You might want to go to dinner and a movie, too."

"But don't you need your car?" I protest.

She shakes her head. "I'm not much for all of that." *Was it love she objected to, or just the public performance of it?* "Something tells me this is going to be a delivery night."

In a few months, Angie and I will break down in her white Mercury Tracer near Okaton, South Dakota—population thirteen. We will pantomime confidence as we climb the interstate shoulder, wait at the rock shop for a tow truck, register with the seedy desk clerk at a frightening and sullen motel. (No IHOPs in sight.) We will then spend the next three nights in the vast metropolis of Murdo, SD, awaiting repairs that cost upwards of $500. Bad gas purchased in Fargo has clogged the fuel injectors. I prefer metaphors: the vital system of the car has gone into shock. Ethanol, a toxin to old engines, has turned the car against itself, weakened its heart.

Back in Bellingham, I am driving to the train station over a crust of snow, wiping the steering wheel at every traffic light. The sweating has gotten profuse, but it's worse in Angie's car, surrounded by her things: stubbed-out cigarettes and a CD by someone named David Gray. I turn on the music. The song is called "Babylon," and as I listen, I miss the turn—not once but twice. Then, I miss it again on purpose. I don't have a cell phone yet. Charlie can't reach me. He'll just have to wait a little while as David Gray counsels me in the quickening dark.

I pull back the quilt on the creaky, South Dakota bed. It's too hot to sleep, I realize, but the sheets are cool, and the TV glows blue as twilight. I tell Angie, "I drove around in your car for an hour that night. I almost drove myself right out of town. I just kept playing that David Gray song over and over. I loved you then, already."

She laughs at me from the tile threshold, the raised line where the carpet gives way: "I left that CD in the car for you. I didn't know if you'd listen to it, but—" water spilling from the shower now, "just in case."

And so it was my biggest U-turn, my most unnerving and necessary change. I no longer need an escape route, but I still keep an atlas snug inside the dash.

•—•

I used to have all kinds of misfolded maps spilling out of the side pockets, clogging the glove compartment. I had an atlas missing its covers from all the times I'd opened it and traced routes along the grids.

I loved going to AAA and getting the TripTiks: those magical accordion books made especially for you, with the best route clearly highlighted in yellow, points of interest and campgrounds circled in green. I took home every map the kind lady behind the counter would relinquish: regional maps, state maps, city maps, national parks. She would wrap it all up in a rubber band and tell me to have a safe trip.

The AAA office always felt so clean, cool, and orderly. Just walking into the white, air-conditioned room made you feel a little more put together, a little more relaxed. Everything you needed to know was organized behind the counter, and any number of women (they always seemed to be women) were glad to help. You could find handy travel gadgets—portable clothes lines! packets of detergent!—that hadn't even occurred to you and now became necessities. You could peruse the luggage, heft the backpacks to assess their weight, though you already owned your perfectly serviceable duffel bag.

My car has that look of people who always drive alone—passenger seat filled with the litter of everyday life: yoga mat, books, receipts, shopping bags. In the back: no child seats, just a layer of dog hair on the blanket, smudges on the window, overturned water bowl. I haven't looked at a real map in ages; I use the GPS on my cell phone, relying on a disembodied female voice to tell me when a turn is coming up, though she sometimes leads me to dead ends. She often says, in a tone that sounds a bit panicked: *GPS signal lost*, and I'll have to keep driving blind. I miss having a real companion beside me, pondering the map, looking out the window, saying, *I think we're going in the right direction.*

Dreams

Night pictures

In my first dream, I am small like the proxy-girl asleep in my bed, and warm like her, too. My dimpled hands clasp the bars of a cage. Am I caged in or caged out, the zookeeper or the beast being kept? It's hard to say. I feel a sense of dread but also of longing. Then, I hear elephants trumpeting in the distance, and as they draw close, I see they are walking single file, their trunks and tails intertwined. They look like elephants I have seen at the circus, enormous and wrinkled, with a silver sheen. Their toenails are painted white as chalk. Their long tusks, like those from the picture books, are missing. Once, I told my grandmother how I rode an elephant at the circus, how I slipped from my seat and crashed all the way to the floor. It was true, but she didn't believe me. She said I must have been dreaming. My parents were there, but they each held a finger over their lips, whispered, *Let's not worry Grandma.*

In this way, my first truth became a lie. Even my witnesses would not confirm my story. In the dream, the bars turn white as the toenails, as the missing tusks of the elephants, and suddenly my hands are clutching, trembling, holding on for dear life. Fear slides down my throat like a soft egg. Am I afraid for the elephants or afraid for myself? Am I safer within or beyond the bars? It is hard to say. For years, my father will tell this story, how I woke him in the dark, crying—how I whispered, *Please, Daddy, the night pictures were very sad.* I remember the dream, but nothing of the waking. Whatever happened after, as with so many stories, I will have to take someone else's word for it.

Of me

For my voice recital, I'm practicing "Dream a Little Dream of Me." It's a sweet melody, and catchy, so I sing it in my head all day long, memorizing the way the bridge swoops up into a high octave, taking all your breath, your faith: *Stars fading...* and then quickly stair steps to a lower register: *but I linger on dear...* Cass Elliot made this song famous in 1968, or maybe it was the other way around: the song put her, and the Mamas and the Papas, on the charts, selling close to seven million copies in an era devoted to political protest songs and drug-induced surrealism. Her voice—strong, yet oh-so-tender—was well-suited for this twenties-era ballad.

She sang it for the last time on July 27, 1974, then two days later died in her sleep. We can't know if she was dreaming when it happened, or what she might have been dreaming of. Perhaps the lyrics still trilled in her head, words like *sycamore*, or *sunbeams*, words that are fun to sing. As I study the song now, I see that the light melody rubs against rather insidious lyrics: the lover insisting, desperately, to be remembered after the night (or the relationship, or perhaps even her life) is over. It's an unrealistic demand, as if you could force yourself into someone's dreams; usually it's the other way around.

Lately, I've been dreaming of my ex-boyfriend, a man I lived with nearly twenty years ago. In the dreams, I'm always chasing after him, or perhaps it's the other way around. We weave down labyrinthine corridors, skim past witnesses who lurk in the corners. He's always just out sight. Sex simmers in the air: either sex we've had or are about to have. Or sex that has failed. Sex that wanted to be love. I wake in a panic, sure that I've done something wrong, an old reproach burning beneath my heart. I blink and I blink my way into the present-day. Which is the lie and which is the truth? It was just a dream, I tell myself, thank God, it was just a dream.

Message from a

Once, when I was fifteen, I dreamed I was following a woman in a white sundress through the aisles of a Thriftway supermarket. Her feet were bare, and I kept thinking how cold they must have been, how dirty their soles. I followed her because she reminded me of Roma Downey, the woman on *Touched by an Angel*—that heavenly ingénue. Monica was her name. I watched her every Saturday night instead of going out with friends. She had red hair and long, slender hands and an Irish brogue. I told myself I was reclaiming my spirituality, reexamining my agnosticism, but really I was just so attracted to her that I ached—a pang like hunger but deeper in the body. I prayed it would go away.

I can laugh now and make jokes about how much I wanted to be "touched by an angel" in the literal sense, but not then. I couldn't have laughed then. In the dream, the woman turns to confront me in the canned food aisle, and I apologize, protest too much, say *I'm not actually following you*, and she raises one of her long, slender hands, places a finger over her lips, and says, *Listen.* Her hair is black, her accent distinctly American, and she doesn't look so much like Roma Downey after all—but I'm still drawn to her in a way I can't explain.

I have a message for you, she whispers. *From God?* I ask, and she nods. Then, right then, my mother is calling for me as if over the loudspeaker in the supermarket, the way she did once when I was a lost child. I say, *Just a minute*, *Mom*, but I can't ever get back to the dream, and every time I pass that Thriftway in real life, I think of the woman, the possible angel, and what she might have said, what message she might have been sent to deliver if there really was a God and if he had taken an interest in speaking to me. Then, one day on the way home from school, I see the Thriftway is on fire. My father is driving, and I hang my head out the window like a dog, watching the firemen with their hoses, the futile spray. *Such a shame*, my father says, as if he knew already and wasn't surprised, as if he always expected the

Thriftway to burn. For many days after, there is ash in the air, and I can smell the building in the distance, smoldering.

I thought it was a

When the 1971 San Fernando earthquake hit, I thought it was a dream. It happened at exactly 6 AM on a school day, an hour before normally my mother would gently shake my shoulder and whisper-sing: *time to get up, dear, rise and shine.* I felt my bed rolling, and thought it was King Kong, a figure I often dreamed about; he stood in my front yard shaking the olive tree, grabbing the fruits in large handfuls as I watched, or he lumbered toward me, swooping me up in his fist to set me in the high branches of the ash tree. From there, I could see my entire neighborhood as if through a fishbowl lens, edges curved and distorted. I'd be frightened, but also exhilarated: to have been chosen, singled out, by something so mighty. So, on the morning of the earthquake, my sleepy mind conflated King Kong with the hand of the earthquake, tipping my bed like a see-saw.

I woke fully to my mother's scream, and saw her blurred figure in my doorway. She wore a white nightgown that billowed around her like a halo. I wonder now how much is memory, how much is fiction, how much is still a dream. Memory often feels like a dream, with a dream's logic, blurred images hovering just on the edge of meaning. We stood huddled in the threshold because that's what they told us to do in the event of earthquake, though nowadays that advice has changed: do not stand in doorways, get under something heavy. Or go outside, away from falling buildings. Or don't go outside, stay where you are. Where I live now, we've been told "the big one" is likely to hit within the next 50 years. In the worst-case scenario, no amount of emergency water will save you. The common wisdom, like memory, keeps shifting, revising. You never know what to believe.

Bring me a

When she came to tuck me in, my mother often sang *Mr. Sandman, bring me a dream, make him the cutest that I've ever seen.* It was the same tune she played on the piano, lyrics we sang together as I perched beside her, learning the simple bass chords. But at night, a cappella in the dark, the song sounded different—less a cheerful ditty and more a bawdy ballad from that grown-up world to which I did not yet belong, might never belong: *Give him two lips like roses and clover, and tell him that his lonesome nights are over!* I always pictured the sandman as our mailman, Mike, skinny and reliable in his blue shorts and button-down shirt, a messenger bag slung across his shoulder. The sandman was bringing me an invitation to sleep, I thought, the same way the mailman brought invitations to parties, postcards from family at the shore. But then this: *Mr. Sandman, I'm so alone, don't have nobody to call my own.* My lip quivered as I slipped beneath the covers, turned over on my side. And I was alone, wasn't I, alone in my small pink bedroom at the end of the hall, alone in my childhood without siblings or schoolmates or neighbor kids with whom to play? Mike told us once he had two daughters, Daisy and Lily, and one of them was about my age. I kept asking my mother where the flower girls lived, but she said they were too far away. Most of the mail that came to our house was for my mother after all. She paid the bills, clipped the coupons, answered all the correspondence with her elegant script. So when Mr. Sandman turned on his magic beam, it only made sense that she would receive the dream.

Life is but a

There are more songs with the word "dream" in the title than you can count. Add in the songs that have "dream" in the lyrics, and it might very well be one of the most sung words in history, perhaps vying only with *moon* and *love.* The vowels in *dream* are actually rather difficult, requiring some modification to avoid a shrill "eee" high up in the back of the throat, like the whine of a mosquito. But I suppose songwriters can't avoid it, that impulse to compare the beloved, or love itself, to a dream, given that love can be so unpredictable and refuses to play by diurnal rules.

Even in our earliest lulls to sleep, dreams are thrust upon us: *Row, row, row your boat / gently down the stream / merrily, merrily, merrily, merrily / life is but a dream.* Sing this to a babe in arms and you impart one of the basic Buddhist tenets: that life, as we know it, is mere illusion. This song is often executed as a round, voices intermingling while vying off one another for dominance. You need to concentrate while singing a round, staying firmly embedded in your part while allowing the competing voices to fade into the background.

Kind of like love, I suppose: voices trying to meet and harmonize, while the lyrics drift out of unison. Rounds are supposed to create beautiful, textured songs—and they're often sung as part of team-building activities, to show that all voices have a part to play—but you can't really *hear* the totality of a round while you're inside it. You have a vague sense that voices are intersecting beautifully, but if you stop to listen you'll lose your way and dissolve in nervous laughter. Whenever I sing *row, row, row your boat*, I imagine a fool jauntily paddling toward a waterfall. He can't see it (his back is turned) though the roar of the rapids rises in his ears. He keeps singing and singing, keeping time with his oars, while the boat tips over into the roiling froth below.

Lover

When we thumbed through catalogs, my mother called the men she found attractive "dream boats." If I was lucky and good and kept myself trim, a dream boat would someday paddle his way toward me. I pictured myself stranded on shore, waiting. When we watched *Lawrence Welk* as a family, my father often whistled at pretty Anacani, then grinned at me: *Wowee, isn't she a dream?* But how could I answer him, really? By then, all the lullabies and bedtime stories had given way to alibis. I spoke in fragments, half-truths, always looking beyond and away. My friend left a Mariah Carey tape in my locker. *You have to hear this*, her note read. I turned the volume way down, pressed my ear to the tinny speaker and heard bawdy Mariah moaning for her dream lover. In her little dream boat, pretty Anacani is always paddling hard. I am always standing on the rocks, screaming her name, but she never hears. Night after night, I wake in terror: both of us, in our own ways, bound for capsize.

Of days gone by

When Susan Boyle took to the stage of *Britain's Got Talent*, no one expected her to succeed. She looked to be the butt of everyone's joke—with her wide face, bushy eyebrows, frumpy dress, and clunky shoes. She said she wanted to be a famous singer "like Elaine Paige." When the first notes of "I Dreamed a Dream" left her mouth, the audience surged with applause; the judges glanced at each other, flabbergasted, and one even started to cry. Was it the mismatch between body and voice that got to them? Or maybe it was just the song itself, its woeful depiction of the gap between fantasy and hard reality.

Now my father is dying in his hospital bed, and we've gathered around, playing songs on my brother's iPhone. It's late, and we've done a lot of work today: a DNR order, a Power of Attorney, a list of myriad transactions that will need to happen upon death. He's tired, lying on his side, eyes closed, gripping my mother's hand. His face is soft, mouth slack. I ask him what his favorite song is, and he says, in a voice that no longer seems to be his voice, *anything from Les Miz.*

This story, *Les Misérables*, is something of a cult in my family; my mother says it's her favorite book and my brother has seen the film twelve times. My parents saw the stage production in London, and they own at least three different DVDs of the musical. I've never seen it myself, but I seem to know the songs by osmosis. My brother finds Susan Boyle belting out "I Dreamed a Dream," the dying mother singing of how dreams must always die, and what made life worth living before everything went wrong. It's not the most uplifting song, but somehow we're all still smiling.

Camera

Frame One: *Light Writing*

Le Gras: a country estate in eastern France. A simple view: rooftops, angles of stone walls leaning toward one another. Niépce had to be a patient man, kept the shutter of his camera open for eight hours to engrave the image on a pewter plate. Or rather, to have the light engrave the image for him. *Light writing*, he called it.

Light writes what it knows. Light has no words, only images. Light composes around its many obstacles.

The camera is a room. A vault, a chamber. In the earliest cameras, men stood inside and let light in through a pinhole. Waiting to see what might develop. Everything depends on that hole and the light that finds its way in.

Frame Two: *The Dickinson Daguerreotype*

At present, only one authenticated image exists of Emily Dickinson. The Dickinson daguerreotype, as her image is known, dates to 1847. The poet was seventeen, as was I the first time I studied her face—earnest and impenetrable, both at once—a young woman of contradictions. Her thin white fingers seem to clasp something—a flower perhaps, or a tangle of thread? Beside her on a table draped with embroidered cloth, the camera has captured the gold-gilt pages of a book. *Who was she reading?*

Dickinson's poems cast a spell on me. They documented the deep and considered longings I wasn't able to express, not yet, not in my daily life at the Catholic girls' school for legacy students and Protestant overachievers. No one had any idea who I was, what I was doing there. I spent hours crouched in chapel after class, writing by the light of tall, stained, clerestory windows.

When we sat for senior pictures against the smudged blue backdrop, its weak conjuring of sky and clouds, I parted my hair in the middle. I brought a dark dress that pleated near the neckline.

"Smile! Smile!" the photographer urged. He had a flashbulb and a busy schedule. He didn't have all day. I let my lips part then, expectant, but I didn't smile. I was waiting for something I could not name.

Frame Three: *Uncompromising Attentions*

Julia Margaret Cameron is in her studio: a former chicken coop that retains traces of its utilitarian origins. Can one ever be fully rid of chickens? She hums to herself as she sets up her camera, adjusts her subject under the skylight that never lets in enough light. She shoots Darwin. Or Tennyson. Or Longfellow. No matter how prominent her subject, she makes each one sit for hours, while she arranges and rearranges. She must be charming, or charmed. They "suffered her uncompromising attentions, and sometimes later compared among themselves the degree of their suffering."

Suffering, as any good Victorian knows, is prerequisite for beauty. The resultant photos show piercing eyes, unruly hair, fleeting expressions caught between light and dark. Tennyson clutches a book, his shoulders wrapped in a shabby cloak. Darwin gazes ruefully toward his chest, perhaps contemplating the elegant logic of evolution, knowing full well that any theory so perfect will eventually cause trouble. Emily Dickinson, years earlier wrote: *Life is a spell so exquisite, everything conspires to break it.*

You can see it in these portraits, but more so in the allegories Cameron composes: she arranges her maid, the neighbor girl, anyone who will stop by, into classical poses of love and loss. They become Madonnas, or Pre-Raphaelite women, or maidens from Arthurian legends. In these tableaus, the focus is blurred, figures shadowed or just emerging from shadow. Cameron develops the prints herself in a darkroom converted from coal storage.

Imagine it: a portrait developing in the dark, smell of earth and mineral in the air. Each face captured in a tenuous frame. Each frame a room in which a subject could be seen in totality. "From the first moment, I handled my lens with a tender ardour," Cameron writes in a letter, "and it has become to me as a living thing, with voice and memory and creative vigour."

Could she have imagined, a century later, the school photographer, huddled under his black cloth? Child after child trooping in, to be captured in the split second of the flash? Then the class photo: students squared up in grid, smiling from their individual frames: teeth missing, bangs crooked, cowlicks out of control. The teacher, stern and beneficent, hub of it all. Wallet-sized photos snipped apart with scissors; a 5x7 set into its frame, all the past selves lined up behind.

Frame Four: *Kodak Moments*

By the early 1990s, my mother had a Canon Sure Shot she could point and click. It was easy to zoom in and zoom out with the micro-lens, which made a pleasant, buzzing sound, then winked like a flirty eye. The shelf in our refrigerator was always lined with film, tiny black canisters with soft gray lids; inside them, 35 mm the size of a spool of thread.

Most children of the later twentieth century developed a Pavlovian response to the phrase *Say cheese!* I was no exception. We learned to freeze mid-bite of cake, mid-rip of wrapping paper, and mug for our mothers' cameras. At first, they were long rectangles with a handle that dropped down, a cord that wrapped around the wrist, and a blinding flash. We saw double for a moment after. The 110 film curved on each side like a Victorian kissing chair I once saw in a museum, then couldn't stop blushing.

At school, our librarian had a fancy camera called a Polaroid, which printed pictures on the spot. Every year I begged Santa Claus for one of those, but the film, my parents warned, was too expensive for a girl who earned merely a dollar a week for her chores.

We all knew what we looked like, of course, so what was the strange allure of crowding together around the table in the check-out room, watching our collective image emerge against the black box, lightening and lightening until we could make out someone's blond hair, green eyes, freckles, a flicker of braces? Each Polaroid picture came with its own frame, a white square margin where Mrs. Olsen wrote "Spelling Bee" or "Field Day" with a fine-tipped pen before pinning the picture to the bulletin board in the hall.

At first, there was such delight in finding a face you recognized, especially when that face was your own. We scoured yearbooks for the likeness of ourselves and our friends. We tore open the envelope of 3x5 prints, which our parents purchased at a separate counter for photo processing at Bartell's. When did the feeling shift to something worrisome, the reflex to shield our faces from the flash?

Once, a girl in junior high told me, "The camera adds ten pounds," like it was nothing, a common fact, and a necklace of sweat soon beaded my collarbone. Surely George Eastman never anticipated my adolescent anxiety, vulnerability, and yes, even my vanity, when, a hundred years before, he began to market the home camera, the first 24-shot rolls of commercial film. I began to read into the phrase *Strike a pose!*, to leave my albums stark and unfinished under the bed, to wonder if every moment of my life was really staged.

Frame Five: *Instamatic*

In 1963 Kodak came out with the "Instamatic" line of cameras. You just had to load the film onto the sprockets (make sure the holes lines up exactly, or you might not really be advancing the film, leading to a series of lost moments), close the back cover, and begin to shoot. This meant everyone could now own and operate a camera, and they did.

My father carried the camera around his neck, or later, at his side, clipped to his belt like a holster. My mother would be plotting pictures before we'd even stepped out of the car. My brothers and I constantly herded together in front of roadside attractions, restaurant signs, or inserted among distant relatives. The word "cheese" stretching your lips, lifting your cheeks into an involuntary smile. Sometimes I said nothing, my mouth clamped shut and full of secrets. Outings became more about documenting the event than experiencing it in the first place.

The "insta" part of "Instamatic" referred to how quickly you could make exposures: shoot, crank, shoot again. The camera knew what to do. You still had to wait days for the prints to be developed; there was still nothing instant about that part of the process. It felt like a surprise: those packets of prints, and the sleeves of cut negatives (that always fell out first, in danger of being lost). Often we looked at the prints right there in the drugstore, under the fluorescent lights, shuffling them like cards to find "a good one." For even with the "automatic" part of the process, there was still great room for human error: a thumb in the way, blinding sunlight, accidental double exposures, some prints mysteriously all black. Often the error lay with the subjects: eyes closed, or pulling a funny face, or flashing devil's horns over an angelic sibling. We had no guarantees, yet always we made doubles.

Eventually my mother glued the photos into scrapbooks or assembled them into collages hung on the wall. So many smiling faces, waves and waves of them. No one really cared about the negatives, so I squirreled them away, holding up the strips to the light: faces with stark eyes, round and white as thumbtacks. Cheshire smiles, floating. All our bodies reversed.

Frame Six: *Röntgen rays*

What about the light that makes its way from inside out, rendering the unseen seen, the invisible visible?

The first X-rays were called Röntgen rays, named for the German physicist who discovered them in 1895. It was the *fin de siècle*, but everything gleamed new and fresh and possible, hardly an end at all. The X-ray—comprised of electromagnetic wavelengths 1,000 times shorter than light—could penetrate soft tissue but not high-density substances, thus allowing bone to be photographed for the first time.

In the dentist's chair, I bite down hard on cardboard, the choking impulse in my throat, my breath tucked like a pocket handkerchief. "Just a little longer," he promises, moving around to the other side, pressing the cold metal camera close to my cheek.

When I am older, I ask to see them—the X-rays of my teeth, the pictures he uses to determine the health of my mouth. What was I expecting? It's hard to say, but I flinch as he places the black-and-white print on the silver tray, regard it through the slats of my fingers.

"You look like you've seen a ghost," the dentist chuckles.

Not a ghost, but a ghoul, a frightening arrangement of roots and spears, the mandible protruding to a menacing sneer. These words slip through my lips before I can strain them: "I'm a monster."

"Well, if you are, we all are," he says, and laughs again.

Years later, I will break my leg in a home accident, what is benignly called a "slip and fall." Most astonishing is the absence of pain, the way my foot merely crooks to the side, limp, and I have no ability to lift it. The break is called "sharp." The break is called "clean." The break is a drawbridge raised—above the ankle and below it—flesh and bone stranded on each side. In the other room, my love hears a sound like shattered glass. "Did you drop a wine bottle?" she asks.

The paramedics say it must be shock. Everyone agrees there should be pain. I wait for it, expectant, clenching my teeth, but the pain doesn't arrive. Instead, a gentle man in green scrubs comes for me. "We need to get your X-rays," he says. In the next room, a lone light flickers, the color of a legal pad.

The nurse covers me with the familiar apron made of lead. I turn to my side, support my body weight, make a quip about all the yoga planks I've done and how they'll finally come in handy. I lift and turn, lift and turn, listening for the monotone, the waves shooting through my skin.

"There's no pain," I reassure him—until the ankle bone drops out, dragging the skin with it, landing on the table with a thud. No pain—and then all the pain at once. Sword after sword of brutal gold light. I am the woman in the magician's trick. The whole room floods white.

Frame Seven: *Ultrasound*

Imagine: the gloaming. That edge between day and night. Dusky, dim, but strangely electric. You wait for something to happen. One bat, then another, appearing, disappearing, erratic. You see them, and then you don't. You glimpse them out the corner of your eye. They navigate by echolocation, but strain as you might you hear nothing but voices on a neighbor's radio, distant traffic like the whooshing of waves. You want to hear beneath it all: the reverberant sound that can lead a creature to its prey in the dark. Sound that can outline any hidden obstacles.

You're nineteen years old and lying on a narrow table in a dark room. Everything is cold: the hospital gown, your bare feet, the ultrasound gel smeared on your abdomen, the round knob of the ultrasound wand pressing on your full bladder. They insisted you drink a full gallon of water before the procedure, as ultrasonic waves travel best through liquid. It's 1978, and only a few decades since they've refined the science of echolocation to find flaws and disturbances in the human body.

Press and click. Out the corner of your eye you see the images fluttering across the screen, but the technician turns the monitor away. In so many films and television shows, there's an obligatory scene of a couple holding hands, watching the first images of their baby appear on the ultrasound. Usually the technician needs to point it out—*there's the head, there's a foot, and oh look! Do you want to know the sex?* Fetuses look otherworldly in these, their first baby photos—monstrous or alien, tucked into a cave of flesh—yet this image brings the warring couple together, all disagreement dissolved. They take a printout home and post it on the refrigerator to remind them what incubates unseen.

But this ultrasound—you, alone, a teenager on a table in a hospital in Eureka, California—does not seek out a healthy baby. This wand wants to locate a defect the way the first ultrasounds detected fatal flaws in metal structures. It wants to know why you're in pain. Press and click. The technician stone-faced. The room so cold.

You will not be given a photo. You'll be rushed to an operating room where they'll excise a growing embryo from your narrow fallopian tubes. You'll have no memory, no photos to document the occasion. You'll have a scar though, a big one, as if you were sawn in half and then stitched back together again.

Frame Eight: ***Ultraviolet***

As a child learning about the sun, you called it "ultraviolent." The teacher slashed through the "n" with her red grading pen, but still you wrote it wrong. "Ultraviolent" made sense to you the way something big and warm and nurturing could harbor a secret rage, could burn with surprising force, could continue to sting in the quiet aftermath for days. The sun was like a mother that way, capable of all kinds of things.

Frame Nine: ***Moon Over Blue Lake***

In college, studying photojournalism, I loved everything about the darkroom: lifting a negative into the enlarger, cropping for the best effect. Dodging and burning to enhance the highlights and shadows. I did all this carefully, intently focused. I swirled the print with my fingertips in the rinsing bath, then clothespinned my photo to the line while I cleaned up, an exacting process. You had to leave the darkroom spotless for the next person, who might be waiting outside, the red light that said *occupied* keeping others at bay. Everyone respects a darkroom.

I once stood on the deck of the house I shared in the town of Blue Lake and watched the moon rise. There was no lake in Blue Lake, just a long, wide valley dotted with softball diamonds. I photographed the moon, made several exposures, experimented with f-stops and shutter speeds. But not until I entered the darkroom would I be able to see what I'd captured.

I should have felt claustrophobic in such a small space, breathless and panicked, but my focus on the prints kept me sane: the images like small windows in a windowless room, letting in the night where I stood so quietly on the balcony, watching the moon rise in the east, watching it all in the viewfinder, already framed. Trying to get just right the bright shadows: a contradiction. How can the darkness be silver, colloidal?

Later, when I hand the finished print to my professor, I think I've finally got it: the balance of elements, a whisper of secrets in the gilded trees and shadows. He sighs and hands it back to me. "This isn't photojournalism," he says, and I get a C+ in the class. I can't seem to simply document.

No, I skulk around at night, making exposures of the most difficult kind. Those redwoods bathed in moonlight, the dark behind them lit from within, and somewhere the owls hooting. Not a song exactly, but a message that sounds silver too, lined with precious metal. That's what I want to capture: *Moon Over Blue Lake*, I'll call it, after Ansel Adams and his wide-angle, black-and-white prints that somehow inscribe distance and intimacy at once. I imagine him by the side of the road in the New Mexican desert, the tripod on the roof of his station wagon: the 8x10 View Camera balanced there, heavy, inscrutable. Light—in motion, transient—writing all of it: the rapport between sky and earth; the empathy of light for dark; umbilicus between a window and its view.

Frame Ten: *Photograph*

I had a locket when I was sixteen. Didn't every girl? Mine was a gaudy gold heart on an oversized chain, and my mother promised someday I would meet a nice boy and keep a likeness of him inside.

A likeness. How I struggled with this word, the almost-not-quite of it, the fondness and the fiction it implied. *Him-but-not-him. Like him but not.*

In school, we studied the photographs Alfred Stieglitz had taken of Georgia O'Keeffe, the woman he thought of as his muse, who later became his wife. She was a subject who could not be made into an object, even naked, even with averted eyes. Her collarbones seemed to slice through the pages, through the film itself. O'Keeffe cut me when I looked at her—*sword after sword of brutal gold light.* She never made me want to look away.

Then the time came when a nice boy and I ducked into the photo booth at the mall. I was looking over my shoulder, squirming out of the frame. All those bright flashes in succession, then the coins we slipped in, the sheet that slipped out, trimmed on each side with a row of tiny holes.

Across my face in every picture, a shadow stretched, flexed; a little swath of darkness, involuntary, instead of a smile. We said we would try again, at a different booth, but the night wore on, and we never did.

Bridges: A Catalog

Whose promises do I
hear from a distant bridge?
—Derrick Austin

(A)

My parents collected *Reader's Digest* Condensed Books: fat volumes that usually held five novels in one. They had faux-leather covers with raised type on the spines, and slick pages full of large-type narratives. The ads for this series featured a bespectacled cartoon reader on the run, book to his nose as he jogs down the street: *My pace is so fast*, he says, *that I am glad to have many of the world's current books delightfully compressed for me by the world's most skillful literary condensers!* The series started in 1950, a time that most of us would not consider "fast" by any modern standard, but I suppose the need to abridge our lives has always been with us.

I often picked up these volumes and flipped through the pages, but it seemed too noisy in there: too many voices in one place. Though the texts had been shortened, their cohabitation made me nervous. Besides, I'd always wondered about the excised parts; hadn't they been necessary? Weren't they bridges leading from one thought to the next? Without them, weren't we in danger of falling?

Bride

Once, as a child, I left my parents an angry note in my best, new, self-conscious penmanship. I meant to write "bride" but wrote "bridge" instead, a keystroke error I still often make when I type. My parents kept the note in a scrapbook, artifact they hoped we would laugh about someday:

If I ever become a bridge: I will not change my name and you can't make me!

Burned

Even a torch carried the wrong way can start a fire. Even a heart committed to love can go hopelessly haywire. I crossed bridges timidly all my youth, clasping my mother's back-stretched hand—but dawdling, too, so she had to pull me hard to bring me with her, to bring me up to speed. More often than not, her anger fueled our journeys; more often than not, I was afraid. *Would we have enough to pay the toll? Would someone mistake my mother for the Troll?* Years later, I saw a flicker of something, her face in my mirror, a chance to change roles, to put—as she used to say—*the fear of God in someone.*

Suddenly, every stick was a match, every wish was a flint, and I was on fire. A friend called to say she was marrying a man she had only just met, and would I buy a dress I didn't like with money I didn't have, and please would I travel across the country to stand before my uneasy past and deliver a blessing for their future?

I was living with a woman I had loved for many years, and the law insisted no marriage for us. Forget about the fancy dress; make no mention of the gifts and certainly not of the dancing. I should have put down my stick and stepped away from the flint. I should have let the scorched receiver cool awhile in its cradle before I called her back. But I had been burning so long in silence. Like the best of magicians, and the worst of friends, I made everything go up in smoke.

Brooklyn

After the planes struck and shut down one of the busiest cities in the world, many people found themselves walking home across the Brooklyn Bridge—covered in ash and debris. Some might have been bleeding; others limped; many were shell-shocked, eyes staring straight ahead. It might have looked like Exodus; I imagine orchestral swellings accompanying them on their flight, but of course they would have heard only their compatriots' footsteps, sirens, the roar of boats beneath the bridge.

The Brooklyn Bridge opened in 1883, spanning the East River, connecting Brooklyn with the island of Manhattan for the first time. It took 14 years, 600 workers, and 25 deaths.

A few months after the attack, a survivor said in an interview that she couldn't bring herself to throw away her clothes from that day. They reeked of smoke, a huddled pile in the corner of her bedroom. *Why can't you let them go?* the interviewer asked. *I don't know*, she said, *I just don't know.*

Caring

An acquaintance recently died of metastatic breast cancer. I'd met her only once, but her vibrant presence gave me the illusion that we'd been the best of friends. She'd set up a journal on the website CaringBridge, where she shared with us the process of treatment, then the cessation of treatment, and then even the dying itself.

A woman developed CaringBridge after her friend gave birth to a premature baby; it's now become the number one personal connection site for those in the throes of crisis. Its mission: *To amplify the love, hope and compassion in the world, making each health journey easier.*

My friend shared how her family was weaving a casket out of willow branches—a "basket casket." She would be carried from her home in this woven bridge. At one point, after a long post in which she detailed the minutiae of her days—days in which time both expanded and contracted—she wrote: "Dying is perfect."

City of

When we first moved to Pittsburgh, my beloved and I were greeted more than once with this blanket declaration: *The City of Bridges Welcomes You!* Bridges were a point of local pride, like Heinz ketchup or 84 Lumber or pretty green bottles of Rolling Rock beer. But just *how many* bridges, I wanted to know, and a fact book in the library informed me: 446. "Think about it," my new boss said. "This is a delta, three rivers trisecting the land. Without bridges, there'd be nothing but a bunch of isolated villages and valleys."

Bridges became my currency in a place where I knew no one but the one I came with. I collected their names like coins crowding a once-empty pocket. We were lonely for bridges of easy camaraderie, for people who didn't ask "partners in what?" or "where do your parents live?"

If I could name them all by sight—the Andy Warhol Bridge, the Rachel Carson Bridge, the yellow Smithfield Street Bridge with its gas lights aglow, or the green Birmingham Bridge spanning the skyline like a monochrome rainbow—if I could point to my favorite one, the industrial Hot Metal Bridge, and say, "Doesn't that remind you of a jungle gym we used to climb on the playground?"—then maybe I could belong to the Keystone State after all. We quizzed each other. Eventually, we could even say "keystone" with confidence, knowing exactly what we meant by the word.

Crane, Hart

"And I have been able to give freedom and life which was acknowledged in the ecstasy of walking hand in hand across the most beautiful bridge of the world, the cables enclosing us and pulling us upward in such a dance as I have never walked and never can walk with another."

Deception Pass

When I first moved to Washington, I visited Deception Pass State Park on Whidbey Island. Well, actually, the bridge enables this park to exist on two islands at once: Fidalgo and Whidbey (are islands connected by bridges still islands? I've always wondered). It's one of the most scenic bridges in the world, and tourists by the hundreds get out of their cars to walk along the narrow edges, wind buffeting their hair. Cars crawl by, their side mirrors just inches away, many of the drivers distracted by the views of the Strait of Juan de Fuca to the west, Cornet Bay to the east. And below it all: the deep current, barely visible on the surface, where unsuspecting boats, expecting an easy passage from one place to another, might perish. Thus, the name "Deception."

I've walked every trail in that park, but no longer leave my car to walk along the high expanse. Many people have jumped to their deaths from this bridge, the pull of all that open space just too great. I stay at ground level, admiring the Madrone trees and their shedding bark, walking at the edge of the bluff. A Salish mermaid totem greets me every time; her story one of bodily transformation, from one element to another.

Dental

Shortly after I moved to Bellingham, I broke a tooth eating a burrito. It was one of those silly accidents: a canine slipping against a molar. My dental insurance from work hadn't yet kicked in, so I lived with the pain for three weeks before seeing a dentist. He tried to save the tooth—root canal, crown—but eventually told me I had two choices: a bridge or an implant.

A bridge is a false tooth held by a wire that spans the gap left by your extracted rotten canine. You need to care for it like a pet: removing it at night, cleaning it with Polident. It would make me feel old, indentured; my bridge effervescing in a glass on the nightstand. So instead, I chose the implant, a process that would take 18 months: the periodontist drilling into bone, screwing in hardware, creating a specialized porcelain crown. We had to pray it didn't fail, which it did, the bone around the implant secreting away so we had to start all over again.

Fifteen years later, the implant holds, but the crown has deteriorated. The dentist tells me they don't make parts for "these old implants" anymore. They search around and finally find a retired periodontist who makes the parts in his garage. "Don't worry," he says, "we'll get you tuned up good as new."

Dickinson, Emily

"Faith is the pierless bridge supporting what we see unto the scene that we do not."

Draw

In Florida, the bridges are called causeways. They are often pink and always crowded. We hardly notice them until they begin to rise. Then everyone is rushing, drivers and pedestrians alike. The red signals flash, the shrill alarm sounds, and the hinged arms descend to remind us there's a half-hourly consequence for following every road to its easternmost end.

"Just wait till there's a hurricane," says my friend who grew up here. "They leave all the bridges up, and the tenders abandon their towers. If you don't evacuate when you have the chance, you'll find yourself cut off from the mainland."

Floating

Around Seattle, locals call it "the Evergreen Bridge" or "the 520 Bridge." One school day I will learn it is the longest bridge of its kind in the world, and I'll puff with pride—as if I had something to do with it—those 7,580 feet of floating road.

But right now I love the bridge for other reasons: it's the way we travel on holidays to visit Aunt Linda.

"When I grow up," I announce from the back seat of our practical car, "I'm going to live in a skyscraper and drive a Mustang convertible." In short, I want to copy everything my lovely aunt has and does.

"Don't you think you might feel a little cramped, with your whole brood inside a small apartment?" My grandmother smiles and pats my knee. We are back seat companions.

Before I can answer, the road slopes down, and my father makes his perennial joke about Jesus. "This is the closest we'll ever come," with a grand gesture, "to walking on water." My mother is uncharacteristically quiet on these trips, perhaps because she is afraid of bridges. She fears high winds and fatal collapse.

Eventually, the Evergreen Bridge will be closed because of poor construction and seismic risks. Repairs will be costly and take far longer than anyone expects. My aunt will die young from breast cancer, separated from all of us by a lake and a long, snaking line of commuter traffic. After this, we will each mourn in our own way, and no one in my family will ever travel to the east side of the city again.

But back then, in that other time, almost a fable, my father likes to reminisce: "You know, there used to be a toll to pay for crossing this bridge. They stopped collecting when it was paid off, turned the toll booths into bus stops." He winks at me in the rearview. "That was a good year. That was the year you were born."

Gephyrophobia

A couple years ago, a bridge collapsed on the major interstate just 20 miles south of Bellingham, Washington. An oversized truck clipped the supports, and shortly after it crossed, the whole span collapsed, bringing down three vehicles with it. (I-5 is one of the busiest freeways in the state; the fact that only three cars sailed across the bridge at this time is highly improbable.) It's everyone's nightmare: the ground crumbling beneath you, the yawning abyss where there should be something solid. Those drivers must not have had time to slam the brakes before their cars drove right over the edge into the Skagit River. Miraculously, no one was hurt; everyone climbed on top of their cars to be rescued.

But for weeks afterward, everyone in town felt shaky, though nothing had happened to us. The Department of Transportation quickly set up detours that worked just fine, but no one wanted to venture more than a few blocks from home. It was as if the bridges, as we always suspected, had been held up by belief alone.

London

It was one of the first songs I learned to play on the piano, eighth notes gliding over the treble clef like junior acrobats with a net splayed wide beneath them.

Why was the bridge falling down in the first place, I wondered, and who is the "fair lady" in whom the minstrel confides? Does she hold the power to repair it? On the playground, Amanda Label and Shannon Binford, best friends since always, lace their fingers and make an arch with their hands. They have long, lustrous hair that they braid for each other. They share headbands and scrunchies, bracelets and rings, even Chapstick—the cherry red kind. One girl presses the stick to her lips, then passes it to the other, a kind of transitive kiss.

This game is better than "Ring Around the Rosie," hopscotch, or tetherball because one day the bridge falls down around me, and I am locked, flushed and grinning, between their soft arms with the stunning green veins.

Lorde, Audre

"Oh bridge my sister bless me before I sleep"

Oakland Bay

In the 1989 Loma Prieta earthquake, an upper section of the Oakland Bay

Bridge collapsed, killing one person: 23-year-old Anamafi Moala. Because both Bay Area baseball teams were playing in the World Series, traffic had been lighter than normal on the span. On an average day, the estimated deaths would have totaled over 300.

When I heard of it, I was living in Seattle, a thousand miles north. But I knew that bridge, had crossed it hundreds of time. It's a long bridge that gives you plenty of time to get anxious, if you're inclined to be anxious on bridges. I imagined what it would have felt like to experience the shaking as one traveled at freeway speed, the water of the bay glaring in the autumnal light. Would you even know what was happening as it happened?

Of Madison County

Robert Kincaid is a photographer for *National Geographic* on assignment in Iowa. He is compiling a photo essay on bridges. Francesca Johnson is a housewife whose husband and children are away at the fair. She doesn't trust him at first. A bridge sets in motion their brief love affair when Robert stops at the Johnson farmhouse to ask directions.

My mother reads the book, declares it smut, hides it in her nightstand drawer. As soon as the movie's out, she and my father rent it from the video store. At fifteen, I am home alone, thinking I'll be helpful—*be kind, rewind* after all. I watch the movie, twice. My heart comes undone, unravels like a ball of yarn inside my chest. I want Robert and Francesca to be together always. I want someone who isn't my mother to wash my hair in the bath. To this day, covered bridges make me blush—the red ones especially.

Over troubled water

I listened to this song constantly when I was twelve years old, a girl alone in her bedroom. Not really a girl nor a teenager; they call it "tween" now, but we had no word for it then: that in-between phase when you are neither one thing nor another. You need a bridge to help you cross over the gaps. I crooned along with Art Garfunkel as he morphed from human being to infrastructure, laying himself down across the rapids. I imagined him as a wooden suspension bridge, with handrails made from polished branches.

The song has sold over six million copies, making it one of the most popular tunes in history, though its five-minute length would normally have made it unsuitable for pop radio. I suppose many people need a bridge, or yearn for someone to offer that kind of assurance. Yet, to me, it always sounded like a song offered as consolation prize ("we can still be friends") in lieu of love. Shortly after the release of this, their bestselling, album, Simon and Garfunkel began drifting apart, and finally broke up to go their separate ways.

Poet

On Westminster Bridge in London, I met a man with a lantern sitting on a tiny stool. He looked weathered as a seafarer, enchanted as a fairy tale. "I'm Joseph Marinus," he said, and shook my hand. On his lap I noticed a stack of colorful envelopes. "These are my poems. Pay whatever you can." Bashful about my American voice, I smiled silently and slipped him a pound. He chose the envelope for me—blue, "to match the color of your eyes." I still have the poem from Joseph Marinus. It's a sweet lyric sketched in fine black calligraphy, but of course, like every once upon a time, when I went back to find him, he was gone.

These many years later, I catch a headline in my hometown news: *Seattle to pay poet to live in a bridge.* This isn't a hoax: *The City of Seattle wants to pay someone $10,000 to live part time in the Fremont Bridge's northwest tower and write poetry.* Friends post links on my Facebook wall. *Come back!* they say. *Be the poet in the bridge! Haven't you been waiting your whole life for this?* But I am older now, no longer lonely and given to roam. Even short trips without my beloved are hard. Still, I print the article and pin it over my desk. I conjure Joseph Marinus as I don my secret smile. A spokesperson for the Seattle Office of Arts & Culture explains—*the hope is that the artist's time on the bridge will help the rest of us understand its place in our city's life.*

Pose

In Sanskrit, Bridge Pose is called *Setu Bandhasana*, which translates literally as "construct a bridge." While the pose appears rather simple from the outside—the practitioner lies on her back, with feet flat on the floor, then lifts the hips until the torso becomes like a slanted board—it can actually be quite challenging. The feet must remain engaged, the shoulders tucked under, the core firm, knees pointed straight ahead. Sometimes we squeeze a block between our thighs to maintain proper alignment. The buttocks grow involved, as do the quads, and the thymus gland becomes stimulated to keep your immune system firing. If you feel yourself coming down with something, Bridge Pose can be an excellent antidote.

Bridge requires you to become vulnerable; you present your soft belly to the world, after all. And, as with so many yoga poses, Bridge requires attention to the breath—breath steady as girder. According to *Yoga Journal*, Bridge Pose highlights the essence of yoga: "While the goal of practice is to realize our connection to the divine Self, the Self is also the bridge to reaching that goal." In other words, the Bridge is a bridge to the bridge.

Rainbow

A rainbow looks like a bridge, with its spanning arch, the illusion that the polycolored light begins in one place and ends in another. So we can be forgiven for believing—as multiple cultures do—that the rainbow is a literal bridge between heaven and earth; between God and human; between immortality and mortality. When a pet dies, it is often said to have *crossed the rainbow bridge.*

Off the shores of Lake Powell, where I lived one year, there's a famous rock formation called Rainbow Bridge. It is not multicolored, but gets its name from its perfect arch. The Navajo called it "a rainbow turned to stone," and it is one of the highest natural bridges in the world. I approached it by boat and by foot, following the trails until I stood at its base. The stone is impressive, but more so the hole underneath. The absence of rock is what makes this bridge a bridge. You are nothing underneath it, barely a speck. You can walk right through to the other side.

Suspension

The strongest bridges have vertical suspension cables so their load-bearing decks don't wobble, no matter how strong the wind. But my life has been like the mountain bridge, suspenders made of rope and not of steel. The boards beneath my feet are rough-hewn wood, green with lichen and dusted with wayward seeds. The bridge shakes with every step I take, but the view from here is not to be missed.

I once believed whatever I was told—angels and devils, salvation and sin, a world that could be parsed like walnut shells. But disbelief, too, is a kind of bridge, which I surely must have known all along. Think of the language that supports them both—the road's traffic mirrored by the heart's. Think of the *falsework*, which is really what it's called: temporary structures made to hold a thing in place until construction is sufficiently advanced for the thing to support itself. Think of scaffolds, which were never meant to last.

Water under the

When we forgive someone their trespasses, we often invoke a bridge and the water that flows underneath. It wouldn't make sense to excise the bridge from that statement, to say instead, "No worries, it's just water," though that is exactly what we mean. We mean that time, life, the world moves oh-so-forward in a current that's inexorable. We can't hold onto anything, no matter how much we try.

But we need the bridge as a reference point between past and future. We need to be able to look upstream—at the water coming toward us, white foam at the surface as it roils over rocks—then turn to watch the water's backside, rushing away. We drop in a twig to trace the water's passage. We are suspended—neither here nor there, neither at origin nor destination.

Wilder, Thornton

"There is a land of the living and a land of the dead, and the bridge is love, the only survival, the only meaning."

Speaking of Sex

"No man buys the cow if he can get the milk for free."

Which is to say that you are the heifer here. Which is to say that you are twelve going on thirteen going on terrified that you will end up living a whole, virtuous life in your parents' basement, sitting between them in church at 45 in a frill-collared dress with strings like an apron, forever unmilked and unmilkable. At this age, though, you are still unsure of the precise meaning of milk in the parable. The apple was sin, plain and simple. The mustard seed was modest beginnings. But sex still seems an extension of kissing to you, kissing with the lights out perhaps, or kissing for a long time in a car. How will you know when you've gone too far, when the milk is spilled, when the virtue is lost? Worse: *what if it never happens at all?*

Your mother appraises you with new suspicions. She sees how you are green for twelve, sheltered for thirteen, yet tall as a grown woman already, your hips coming in hard and strange as teeth. "This changes everything," she sighs, making a mixture of salt and soap, filling the sink with water that scalds her hands. You are known for grass stains and mud stains, the blackberry juice on your first pair of pure white Keds. *Why is blood so different?*

You think she can hear your thoughts, even this one, words dangling over your head like worm-bitten fruit. You stand barefoot at the threshold, big bag of Kotex like a toddler at your hip. You are fidgeting. You are biting your lip. You are afraid your father might walk in, and if he does, you will see his thoughts flash like traffic lights, his silent disappointment and fear.

"From this day until the day you're married," your mother says, and she is scrubbing now, furious and determined, "you can never let your guard down again."

•—•

"Slut. Tramp."

You've let down your guard. You're walking to school, as always, on a Monday, a rare smile gracing your face. But then you see the scrawl, before you can make out the words. Black paint dripping down the face of the gunmetal locker, right above the combination lock where every day, for three years, you've placed your fingers just so to open. Inside sit your books, neatly stacked—World History, Algebra, Shakespeare—and the centerpiece you've made for Home Economics. Paper flowers out of tissue paper, gathered together with a raffia bow.

But now, those words. Ugly words. What have you done to deserve them? You try to think quickly back to the weekend: whose boyfriend did you kiss? Who held your hand? But it's a blur of laughter. Of fumbled buttons and heads turned away.

You're a good girl, everyone knows that. You always do what you're supposed to do. Honors student. Straight A's. But something happens on the weekends: desire gets a hold of you and won't let go. There's a song on the radio: *She gets too hungry for dinner at eight…* And that's what it feels like, a hunger that can't wait. But even that hunger feels appropriate. Sanctioned.

You turn away from the locker, from the words, and go to your Home Ec class empty-handed. The teacher glares at you, asks how you could have forgotten? Now the perfect table is ruined, and all the girls look at you, their gazes hot, like irons. It will be years before you understand the rest of the lyric: *She never bothers with people she hates, that's why the Lady is a tramp.*

•—•

> "Young people who are well adjusted, highly motivated, and future oriented are far less likely to be sexually active than those with a low self-concept and low ideals. The commandments listed on this page are meant to be a guide. Use the checklist below to help you formulate your **personal commandments** about what you will and will not do as you grow toward sexual maturity."
>
> —*Sex and the Teenager* (Ave Maria Press, 1990)

Your all-girls Catholic high school doesn't offer sex education class. There is a dubious unit at the end of Health called "The Female Body" during which Mrs. Boyle reviews the diagram that looks like a cow's head with two droopy ears, then tests the class on the names of all the things inside them. You get an A- because you confuse the ampulla and the isthmus of the uterine tube. Key words you are waiting for—*love*, *desire*, and *orgasm*, especially—are never mentioned.

In World Cultures, the syllabus allocates eight weeks to study Christianity, three for Judaism, three for Islam, one for Other Religions of the World, and a final week for "Contemporary Moral Issues," which is a euphemism for "Don't Have Sex Until You're Married." If Ms. Curran's eyes had been less green, or her taste in clothing less impeccable, you might have pointed out the clear bias toward Catholic theology in this class as well as the obvious favoritism shown religions with only one god.

Instead, you spend hours after school inventing credible reasons to visit Ms. Curran in her office.

By the time you read *Sex and the Teenager*, you are running out of them. You tell Ms. Curran you need help drafting your list of personal moral commandments, but when you show up after school with notebook in hand, she calls your bluff.

"Since when do you need help writing anything?" Her mouth is smiling, but her eyes say, *Enough with the bullshit already.*

You have to think fast. She is leaning across the desk in a plum turtleneck and a camel blazer with elbow patches. Her eyes are the color of olives. Suddenly, you blurt out: "You know back in the Judaism unit when we watched *Yentl*? Well, Yentl is pretending to be a man, right? And she marries Hadass, a woman. And even though she tells her they don't have to do anything… you know… *marital*… if they did—because they're both actually women—would it *count*?"

Ms. Curran slides back in her chair. "As what?"

"As *sex*?"

A dent forms between her eyebrows. Finally, she says, "I think a better question would be, *As sin*?"

You each wait for the other to proffer an answer. Twenty years later, you are still waiting for that silence to break.

•—•

"Was it good for you?"

You. Yes, you. Was it good? Good the way he pats the bed, welcomes you there. *Come to bed…* Good as in *Godly.* The prayer said in bed. A prayer that accelerates, invokes the almighty: *Oh God, oh Jesus, Yes!*

Take off your clothes slowly, or quickly, depending on the mood, the lighting, how scared you are, what color panties you're wearing, what shape your bra is in, and have you recently shaved your legs, your pits, trimmed your bush, sculpted yourself into something smooth—a thing that has no rough patches—oil up the elbows, exfoliate the face, pluck every hair from your chinny chin chin—you are slick, you are warm, you are good.

Come in, you say, no need to knock. *Knocked up*, they call it, as if someone knocks on the door of your womb—Come in!—or huffs and puffs and blows the house down.

What you really wanted, what made it *good*, was a mere finger or a tongue slid up the spine, touching that dime-sized spot between your shoulder blades—a spot like a migrated g-spot: so sensitive, exquisite, almost painful—a spot you could never reach on your own. Everything else you could manage, but this… this inaccessible place, nestled just out of reach… you need another body, you almost beg, *please*, *please*, *please*, while the tongue slides up each knob of vertebrae, until you moan: *yes. there, right there, oh God, so good.*

•—•

"I'll have what she's having."
—*When Harry Met Sally*

You were ten when the film debuted. You saw it a decade later. Then, you started having sex, which is also when you started faking it. You, yes you. After all those years of research, from the "S" encyclopedia in fourth grade to D.H. Lawrence in college, you had been longing your way toward it—the coveted title, "sexually active" at last!—only to come up short, disappointed. In your journal you wrote, *You're so passionate. What's your problem?* But then you feared someone might find your journal—that *he* might—and so you burned those pages over the soap dish. Paranoid much?

You, yes you: late-bloomer, condom-hoarder, pamphlet-reader at Planned Parenthood. You were so prepared you could have been a Boy Scout. Why not a badge? But hadn't you been promised a rose garden? A champagne cork popping and waterfalls and fireworks, a veritable tsunami of pleasure?

Your biology teacher told you once that the best approximation of an orgasm was a sneeze: that pent-up feeling, persistent tickling, rapid breathing, accelerated heartrate, followed by a satisfying release. But if that was true, why did sex for you feel like cleaning your ears—or more precisely, having them cleaned: the pressure, the probing, a sense of a tunnel with no end and no light. But if you could just get through it, you could have pancakes. You could sit together in your couch-bed, watching reruns of *Mary Tyler Moore*.

And you, yes you, were such a good girlfriend. You always said yes. Indoors, outdoors, showers, sofas, the stock room at work, even the freight elevator once. You always smiled, always kissed back. You studied up and tried harder, like there was a brass ring to reach, or an A+ to earn, you with your Protestant work ethic, your dream weaver on the door knob, your sheaves of love poems that captured precisely what you did not feel.

You kept at it, even when you broke out in rashes (*a burn from his beard? an allergy to his aftershave?*), even when your roommate said, "This is awkward, but I have to ask you about the bruises..." You came home blue and purple, but nothing hurt. He didn't hurt you. To this day, you don't know why you turned colors like that. You closed your eyes and tried, then wished, then prayed, *Oh God!* Then you gave up and pictured the best deli sandwich you'd ever had.

•—•

"Use it or lose it."

You're in the gynecologist's office, squirming in pain. You never like being here (who does?) but she needs to scrape the cervix to see if any precancerous cells have taken up residence.

It's been two years since you've had a period. They silently disappeared without your really noticing it. No hot flashes; no night sweats. Just a gentle cessation.

And a cessation, too, of your sex life: it vanished with nary a goodbye, a "see ya," or a "take care." Just crept out on tiptoe, carefully closing the door with a barely perceptible click. You weren't paying attention. After ten years you look up startled from your oatmeal and realize it's gone. You thought it just went out for a pack of cigarettes, a jug of milk.

Lately, you've been dreaming of getting your period at inopportune times: when lost and confused in a new place, searching for where you're supposed to be. The blood appears, and you're unprepared, have nothing to staunch the flow.

The doctor gets out the smallest speculum she can find, the kind made for a child. "I'm sorry this is causing so much pain," she says as she inserts the blades, makes that first crank to separate them (the harsh *click… click* that always makes you jump). But even this is too much, and you can't suppress the *ow, ow, ow* blurting from between clenched teeth. The nurse holds your hand, pats a shoulder.

The doctor withdraws quickly, tosses the speculum in the sink. When she uses the word "atrophy," she says it quickly, scribbling in your chart. She prescribes a hormone cream, reschedules for six weeks later. "It's common," she says, "for a woman your age," patting your leg on the way out the door.

•—•

"Vanilla."

The first time you hear the word you think the girls are talking about baking. You remember a small brown bottle you clasped as a child, inhaling so deeply your eyelids drooped, your mouth went slack, the sigh of an older, more experienced woman escaped your lips. Your mother, the baker, seemed indifferent to all of this. She snapped her fingers when she wanted it. She poured a teaspoon of the dark liquid into the batter. Then, she told you to tighten the cap, wipe down the sides, and return it to the right place on the shelf.

But the girls in the college lounge are not talking about baking. They refer several times to a place called Lovers Package, where you can buy costumes and handcuffs and edible underwear, some other gadgets you don't quite understand. And they know it. They say, "This kind of thing isn't for everyone," and smile in a way that makes you wince. One of the girls wants to drive to Seattle to a sex-positive club. She talks at length about being whipped, how good it feels to surrender control. In the corner chair, you eat your Red Vines quietly, try to concentrate on the book in your lap.

"It's not that there's anything wrong with being vanilla," another girl says. She casts you a less-than-subtle glance. "But it's like—come on—kiss, kiss, touch, touch—so much tenderness. What am I supposed to do with that?"

You have a few ideas, but you keep them to yourself. You are grateful for kissing and for touching, but so far the exhilaration seems to come more from your head (*This is really happening!*) than your skin. You don't know how to untie the visceral knots, and no one else seems to know either. In a few years, you will meet someone who can lay a hand on your wrist or the crook of your arm and send a ripple of heat through your whole body. When you slide into bed with her, your mind will quiet for the first time, maybe, ever. You won't have to think so hard about everything now—what is "natural" or "normal," what feels good, least of all how vanilla you are. Her scent will enfold you like a second pair of arms. Your eyelids will droop, your soft mouth slacken. The sigh that escapes will rise from a place you do not recognize, taking you both by surprise.

•—•

"Woman Seeking Women"

It's surprisingly difficult to change your profile on Match.com, to have it accurately reflect who you are and what you really want. You've already put up the photos of you with your dog, of you traveling to interesting places (Switzerland! Palm Springs!), of your dog by herself illuminated in the evening sun, as if her sacred beauty somehow reflects your own. You've put down your interests ("cooking, film, reading"—holding back the "eating, television, solitaire"). You've characterized your body type as "about average," though sometimes you're "athletic and toned" and sometimes you're "a few extra pounds." You are never just one thing or another.

But Match insists that you are. They insist you are either a "woman seeking men" or a "woman seeking women." There is no drop-down category for the fuzzy area in between.

Your profile has been up for years as a "woman seeking men between the ages of…" (that number shifts from year to year, inching up, as you deliberate how low you can go without seeming imprudent, though men don't seem to worry about that, so many of them, no matter their age, seek women "between the ages of 21–35.") And whenever you do a search, hundreds of men pop up on your screen, smiling out from their little boxes—some shirtless, some with baseball caps, often wearing sunglasses.

So many possibilities, but nothing ever pans out. You can't seem to let down your guard. You can't seem to remember what it's like to be with a man—laughing, joyriding in the dark. All you can remember are the late-night fights, or worse, the endless silences, the too-familiar gaze of disappointment.

All you have to do is change the category to "woman seeking women." It's a simple click of the mouse. You know you want to do it, have already been thinking of those times, years ago, when you were with women, the pure sensuality of it: the way their tongues and fingers needed no guidance. The way you let down all your barriers and sighed with pleasure. But you were so young then, and your body flexible. No atrophy, certainly not.

But will the Match women see you as a dilettante, an imposter? Will they be able to see your search history, your past? All you want is someone to see you for who you are. When you do it—when you make the tiny revision—the women appear, but not many. Not as many as the men. They smile from their little boxes, women with short hair and long; women with dogs; women waiting for you.

•—•

"Playing for the other team."

There will be sex. In the beginning, so much sex you are always stumbling out the door, poorly dressed and reeking of cover-up perfume. Sex, but also dishes to wash and waiting for an oil change and taking out the trash. Still sex, more sex, but also student loans and emergency rooms and twice so far, dressing in black and standing together to pay your respects. After a death, the sex is so urgent, eclipsing everything else. You have to touch the one you cannot bear to lose.

It is not *all sex*, as some critics and voyeurs seem to assume. It is not all *play*, and yet, it is not all *foreplay* either.

Your friend from childhood furrows her brow: "Is it mostly a lot of snuggling, like a pajama party every night?" *Not quite.* A woman you just met leans closer and pats your hand: "You must be very resourceful. I can't imagine how you girls *manage* it." Soon, everyone wants their turn to theorize: the ex-fiancé who thinks you're "impressionable," the mother who says you have a "hormone problem," the pastor who writes of your "lost faith," your "Sapphic weakness."

Recently, a senior poet approached you after a reading. "What strikes me," he said, "is the way everything comes down to sex for your people." *You people. Your people.* You might have added the "r" to soften the blow.

Every day you put on your jersey like everyone else. You oil your glove and take a few laps around the diamond. At first, no one can tell which team anyone belongs to, but then the speculation begins: how you hold your glove, how you throw the ball, how deep in left field you're willing to stand.

You want to go back and tell the poet he was wrong. It isn't sex that divides you, though every epithet you've ever heard suggests otherwise: *Muff-diver. Vagitarian.* Et al. It's the loneliness you feel after the game, sipping your drink at the bar. You're always waiting for the other cleat to drop. "I'm not into women," they'll say, suddenly, like an after-thought. "Too bad you're gay. My nephew would love you!" Delivered with such zeal. "I'd like to have you over some time, but my husband's a little conservative." They'll smile apologetically. You know this smile. "Would you mind if I didn't tell him who you are?"

Exercise

Presidential

In 1966, President Lyndon Johnson created the Presidential Physical Fitness Award, a test designed to prioritize exercise in elementary schools. Studies had shown that America's children were out of shape, and so the test included sit-ups, pull-ups, a softball throw, a broad jump, a 50-yard dash, and a mile run. If you scored in the 85th percentile in all categories, you received a badge your mother might sew onto your jacket.

I was eight years old in 1966, a child who really wasn't even aware she *had* a body. I read a lot of books slumped in poor posture on my bed, on the floor, in a kitchen chair, in the back seat of the car. I watched television—*Dark Shadows*, *The Addams Family*, *Get Smart*—lying on my stomach on the carpet, legs scissoring the air behind me. I ate lots of rye toast with peanut butter. I tap-danced for a year, my legs clumsy in the heavy shoes. On the playground, I stuck to the perimeter, doing my best not to be seen, avoiding eye contact with the dodgeball, the handball, any kind of ball whatsoever.

I suppose we heard of the test and perhaps even trained for it, but I have no memory of any kind of preparation. I remember the shriek of whistles, students lined up, all of us shifting in our white tennis shoes to peer over each other's shoulders. We strained to hear the teacher, who held a large clipboard and issued complicated instructions. We—children keenly aware of pecking orders, of the thin line between inclusion and banishment—were suddenly being asked to perform feats of endurance in full view of our peers.

This body: it hardly knew what to do with itself. My arms heeded no direction from my brain. My legs snaked out long and crooked in the harsh light of the sun. My skirt grew frantic with static electricity and clung to my thighs. My knee socks gave up the ghost. My ankles turned inward as if feigning sleep.

The broad jump: alone on the runway, sprinting knock-kneed and then pushing off hard at the line, only to tumble in the sand a foot or so from launch. The pull-up: straining at the bar, every muscle fiber threatening to break, and making not even one. Sit-ups: your partner humming with boredom while watching you contort, your face red and covered in sweat.

The body's failure: it won't be the last time your body is tested and found wanting.

Piano

It was the instrument you didn't have to bring yourself—not like the flute in its slender black suitcase or the guitar with its over-the-shoulder encumbrance. "Many grand places have grand pianos," my mother liked to say. Perhaps there would be one in the parlor of a fancy restaurant or the lobby of a nice hotel. When we browsed the Nordstrom's downtown, she would follow the sound of "Moon River" or "Send in the Clowns," the melody rising like elegant steam through every level of the open floor plan.

At home, I practiced my scales, chords, and arpeggios on a crotchety upright with a wan splash of light above my head. The piano was tucked away in a corner of the basement, where I ventured alone only reluctantly and with a tuba-sized terror in my heart.

"Picture the pianist in the department store," my mother urged. Sometimes this meant a man in a black cutaway jacket with neck tie and tails. He perched on the flat, shiny stool, his eyes closed, his posture impeccable. Sometimes this meant a woman in a long black dress with a scoop neck and a single strand of pearls. One foot pressed down on the damper pedal, and the other kept time with a soft-heeled click. "Don't you want to bring music into people's lives?"

It's not that I was terrible at piano. I practiced my exercises for half an hour each day, then stowed my music inside the bench with the splintery lid. I hid a notebook there, too, so I could work on my stories in between songs. It took several minutes of silence before my mother began to stomp on the kitchen floor. When she did, I'd tuck my pencil behind my ear and resume that dutiful ivory-tickling that meant so much to her.

One year, Mr. Van Lierop made arrangements for his students to play at Rainier Square. It was Christmastime: an evergreen flocked and flashing white lights in the foyer, gold banisters decked with red and green bows. My parents stood in their trenchcoats and scarves like bodyguards someone else had hired. The lid rose high, like an elephant's ear, and the sound traveled admirably through the marbled interiors. I memorized all the notes and played them without error, yet—what would you call it? Something *ineffable* was missing. I heard the hollowness coming from my own hands.

"There was no drama," my mother mourned. "No verve, no urgency, no pizzazz." The ineffable, it seemed, had many names after all.

Later, Mr. Van Lierop, kind intercessor that he was, suggested, "Julie beats to her own drum… And perhaps her drum is not a piano."

I tapped my pencil on my notebook and looked away.

Exorcise

The words are so close, too close—just a slip of the vowel. They do have related etymologies if you're looking for it, that "ex" meaning to drive off or put into motion. And if you're a person battling demons of whatever sort, exorcism is what it feels like when you set your heart rate soaring.

On the treadmill, Bruce Springsteen crooning in your ear, setting the speed to 4.5 miles per hour, the incline to 9, walking fast with your arms ratcheting at your sides, breath rasping, knees twinging. Striding toward it, faster and faster, not sure if you'll make it this time—that moment when it all falls away. When you hit the zone. When you feel like you could keep moving forever, though you're going nowhere—the body and mind finally in sync.

I used to work out with my boyfriend, and depending on the day, we'd do cardio or weights. I did the weights just to please him, to show that I could be strong when the situation demanded it. We left the washed clear light of a Montana afternoon to enter the dim basement of the university gym. Always, there'd be the smell of sweat and cracked rubber, the sharp clang of machines, or the grunts of someone executing free weights on the mat. No one made eye contact except with themselves, focusing on their own bodies in the long mirrors as they did squats or an overhead press.

We would spot each other. There was something vaguely sexual about it: my head facing up to his groin as I did a chest press on the bench, with just a 5-lb. weight on either side of the bar. He kept his fingers curled under the center and urged me to do more reps than I thought possible, barking commands: *you've got it, one more, one more!* I grunted and pushed up the bar one more time while he grabbed it and placed it back on the brackets. My pecs would burn, and later I'd barely be able to lift my arms to wash my hair in the shower.

Once, a professor we knew came over to us as we took turns with the lat machine. I loved this particular round because it involved pulling *down*, rather than struggling up, and I knew I already had well-defined shoulder blades that jutted out on each rep. My arms made a natural wide V, and my back rippled with muscle. The professor watched for a while, and then murmured, *she better be careful, if she exercises too much her tits will get even smaller!* My boyfriend, usually so game for sexual banter, was stunned into silence.

When we broke up, I'd drive to the gym, see his car, and detour to the bottom of the trail that led up to the big white "M" on the hillside. I got out and started moving, sluggish at first, my legs heavy, my stomach in a knot. I'd keep going, walking faster, pushing myself up toward the summit. I kept my gaze on the path. My heart pounded until I thought it would break.

ROTC

Pre-dawn mornings outside my college dorm, I'd hear them: the students training for future military life. I woke early, slipped out of bed and laced up my shoes, lured by the prospect of silence, a quiet place beyond my blaring mind. But soon I had to rise earlier and earlier if I wanted to avoid the rows of serious boys—their crew cuts and steely eyes, their clenched fists and calf muscles bulging as though they would split—while they circled my building, heavy-footed, chanting something about unity and pride.

To my surprise, there were a few female recruits in our school's ROTC program. I watched them straggling behind, their limbs flimsy by comparison, their feet kicking out to the side. A man at the front barked his commands, and the boys complied as if they were one body. The girls—how they tried—but they couldn't keep up. I blushed at these discrepancies. I felt inadequate on their behalf. Soon, I ducked down a side path and went my separate way.

One afternoon, leaving the dining hall, I saw a boy from psychology class. He waved me over to his table, saying, "I know you, don't I?" Did he? Did anyone? I only shrugged and smiled. "But I've seen you running," he said. "Why don't you sign up for ROTC?"

"I'm not a joiner," I told him. His eyebrows were trim and arched as he listened.

"What does that even mean?"

"I like to exercise by myself," I said, more firmly this time. "I don't need any more noise in my head."

"Even for tuition remission?" And just like that, a pamphlet dangled from his hand.

They were running in formation around the chapel in the quad. They were doing jumping jacks and push-ups with their legs spread, then with one hand tucked behind their backs. Some of the strongest boys could even clap between each lift and lower, their bodies transformed into boards. The girls were there, too, shivering against the pavement, still wet with last night's rain, pressing down on each other's feet as they crunched and twisted and scissored their obliques.

And all the while, everyone was shouting, the chill air rising out of their mouths. One harsh syllable marched in line behind another. Then, the boy I recognized: breaking formation, meeting my eyes. I blushed in that moment for all the longing I was missing. I felt inadequate for reasons my own legs could not outrun. Before he could raise his eyebrows or his hand, I ducked down a side path, went my separate way.

Core

Like an apple's. A hard interior that cradles the seed. You gnaw away the juicy flesh, teeth scraping, until all that's left is the core. You throw this misshapen thing into the underbrush.

You do crunches, your partner holding your feet and counting. You do the twisting lateral machine, you do knee raises, and you try to feel a glimmer of it: the core muscles firing. Muscles that normally get to shy away, let other muscles do the work.

In Kundalini yoga, the core muscles are coaxed out of hiding, then flogged. You do the bicycle a hundred times. You sit in an upward V until your entire body shakes and begs to be released. You do the breath of fire, stomach pumping, until all the bad air has been expelled. Afterward, your belly hurts so much you can barely reach for a glass without wincing. It turns out the core muscles connect to everything.

One day you go to your voice lesson, and there's a large inflated medicine ball in the center of your teacher's parlor. You must sit on this ball for the duration of the lesson—45 minutes—your body shifting to find its balance. You do the vocal exercises this way—*ya ya ya ya ya!*—your jaw flapping, tongue settling in its shell. You sing "Somewhere Over the Rainbow," focusing on the core, the way you have to imagine a crochet hook angling up just below your ribs to get your voice to vault over that arch. So many little muscles or tendons move this way and that; you can hardly keep track of them, while your voice billows out of you. The next day, you'll tell people, *I'm so sore from my voice lesson!*, clutching your belly, and they'll look at you strangely, not sure how the voice can be a muscle that is worked.

You bounce a little on the ball, feel the way the thighs support your core, which in turn supports your shoulders and keeps the chest open. And with the chest open, the throat relaxes, the jaw is freed, and your voice spirals to the top of your head, opening the fontanel that closed shortly after your birth.

And perhaps it's a kind of rebirth, a coming home, when you locate your core, when you feel it glowing like an incandescent rod. The core, after all, is the deepest part of you—beyond muscle, beyond bone.

Spin

At the end of season four of the sitcom *Ellen*, the quirky, affable heroine Ellen Morgan comes out. You are a senior in high school at the time, not permitted to watch programs your parents deemed "questionable." You saw the cover of *Time* in the checkout line with real-life heroine Ellen DeGeneres pronouncing, as if with a wink and a shrug, "Yup, I'm gay." You touched the red border of the magazine, then drew back your hand as if from the burner of a hot stove.

Years later, ensconced in your own lesbian life, you watched the *Ellen* series on Netflix. Your partner laughed as she wandered into the room, saying, "I can't believe you've never seen any of this." Season five begins with Ellen on a spin bike, dripping sweat and slipping over the handlebars, gaga for the instructor, who is friendly and fit and praises Ellen for her hard work and enthusiasm. In your head then—a little gong, a sweet ringing song of sudden insight. How had you arrived in your mid-twenties without realizing that gay had never meant happy to you? The few lesbians you had seen depicted in television or film were either suicidal or homicidal, consumed by crippling grief or rage. And the few lesbians you had known in real life were solemn or secretive. They seemed always to be teaching someone a lesson about equal rights or looking back over worried shoulders, fearful of being exposed.

"I think I'd like to try spinning," you said out loud, or maybe you made the resolution in silence. Somehow this activity, paired with Ellen's goofy grin, promised a conduit to a new kind of self-expression. *You were cheerful, and you were gay, just like Ellen Morgan!* You too craved affirmation from those who saw your zeal as valuable, not disingenuous or misguided. Perhaps there was a place for you in Lesbian Land after all.

Now at the Hollywood YMCA, you've gained a reputation as a "hard-core" spinner. You take four to five classes a week and always come early to set up your bike, making sure the seat is raised to just the right height, the handlebars set far enough away from your chest so you can flatten your back completely when you climb. The class rides to Lady Gaga and Jimmy Buffet,

Pharrell Williams and Tina Turner, classic songs and one-hit wonders alike. In real life, you never feel so "part of the pack," such an integral member of the human peloton. It doesn't matter that you're gay here, not in the neon-flashing dark where the sweat of twenty mostly-strangers comingles on the rubber-flex floors. For one hour at a time, you get to forget you're different from most of the people you meet, that a moment will always come when, just by naming your life or the woman you love, you step out into a fragile spotlight, stand there trembling, waiting to be judged.

The spin teacher greets your smile with his own. He approves of your zeal, shares your enthusiasm for the endurance this kind of work requires. He is gay, too, and in his presence, you relax a little, loosen your grip, the coils always so tight in your abdomen, and begin to pedal toward something—a field of wildflowers, say, or a clear mountain lake—instead of always away. "Get on her wheel!" Jack grins, pointing to you, letting you set the up-tempo pace.

You've learned how to harness your breath, how to soften your shoulders and deepen your stretch, how to use your hamstrings and your glutes so as to execute each pedal stroke with your whole musculature. It is joy after all, that propels you to the summit.

Works-in-Progress

First draft

I remember my mother clearing the table, just as she always did. I remember my father opening the newspaper, which was long as a dress back then. His face and lap disappeared behind it. When my mother returned, she always had a project in hand: perhaps a needle and thread to sew a button back on an impish shirt, or perhaps her hot glue gun (*careful! don't touch!)*, poised like a trigger over any chip or crack. In our house, nothing stayed broken or disheveled for long.

For dessert, familiar things: a pad of white pages with a coiled seam and a two-story box of crayons. How I loved opening and closing that box along its cardboard hinge, the revelation each time of a stunning chorus of colors. "Go ahead now—*draw something*," my mother said. She was a teacher, so she knew what children did.

That night, I asked for a pencil instead.

"What do you need a pencil for?" my mother inquired. There are her deep-set eyes, blue as the digits on the microwave clock, flickering with surprise.

My father shifts on his wicker chair; the seams of his paper crinkle. The kitchen smells of meaty leftovers and a floral spray meant to disguise them. It doesn't. This is the first time I can see myself clearly in a memory: I'm four or five, so tall for my age that my feet already scrape the floor when seated. I'm an "early reader" because my mother has taught me what the 26 glorious symbols mean, the sounds they make and the ways they play together.

I can even see her desk in the corner, complete with a seashell box from which at least a dozen pencils protrude. All she has to do is reach behind her and hand me one or grant me permission to rise. I remember the way my pulse climbs my neck like a ladder when I say it aloud: "I want to write something, Mom."

Second draft

My mom has beautiful handwriting, a flow of lines as delicate as her fingers: small knuckles, slender nails, groomed. *You just need to take your time*, she says, coolly, as if that's all it takes to be elegant. Even now, at age 86, her script remains the same, betraying no infirmity of age.

My own handwriting is slipshod, a jerky amalgamation of printing and cursive, hardly intelligible even to my own eye. My father and I shared this affliction. When he was in the nursing home at the end, I found a slip of paper on which he'd practiced writing his own name, over and over, trying to get it right. I wish I'd kept it: these earnest marks he left in his wake.

But years before all that—when my parents are immortal—I sit in my bedroom, the door closed tight against the rest of the house. I don't yet understand the concept of *family*—how fragile it can be, how rare to be safely ensconced. Instead, I sit at my pink desk, stubbornly setting myself apart. I listen to the sprinklers doing their appointed rounds on the back lawn, over and over, a rhythm that ticks *you are here*, *you will always be here*, in Morse code. I'm writing in my diary, a little book with lined pages and a tin lock, but I don't really have anything to say. All language seems to be a code I cannot break.

So I write—in large letters that refuse to stay aligned—all the annoyances I don't dare say aloud. I write, indignantly, that my father sucks his teeth too loudly after dinner. I write how unfair it is that I have to clear the table when my brothers get away scot-free. I write about my brothers: how uncouth they are, how they smell. All my lines are about *feelings*, feelings that make my skin itch and have nowhere else to go. Feelings that are unacceptable.

And this venting really doesn't help. I look out my window, see the way heat rises in waves across the concrete, how water evaporates before it fully hits ground. I close the little book and pretend to lock it with the ineffectual key.

Third draft

I have a red diary with a tiny gold key. I have a huge pink snail called a Keyper—misspelled on purpose!—because the shell is opened with a huge pink key. Sometimes I wear this key on a ribbon around my neck or tuck it inside the zippered pocket of my pillow. I want to have something worthy of a Keyper, a secret important enough to stow away, to keep "under lock and key." That's when I realize—language has always been my secret.

Some kids collect bottle caps or baseball cards or caterpillars in jam jars with holes poked through the top for air. Some collect more unusual things, like my friend who pilfers colored rubber bands, then sorts them all by hue. Someday she hopes to have enough for a full elastic rainbow. What I collect are words, invisible to everyone but me. But what if I got a concussion, say, or that amnesia so prevalent on daytime TV? My words would be lost without a bread crumb trail. No one would even know that they were missing.

So I take a piece of notebook paper and begin to inventory what is most important to me. First the word itself, in the left-hand margin, printed small enough so it barely touches the long red line; then various meanings of the word, as I have encountered them, strung together with semi-colons that dangle like Christmas lights.

Sometimes I use a word in a sentence, placing it between two parentheses. That's when I smile to myself and underline the <u>parent</u>—another part of my collection, these words within words—which lead by ellipses toward metaphors… how I, an only child, find myself perched between my parents on the sofa, <u>parented</u>, <u>parenthetical</u>, set apart <u>inside</u> the brackets of their bodies but also <u>aside</u>, like something you say in a whisper, not meant for everyone to hear. I am my parents' whisper.

It goes on like this: each word or symbol—which can also be spelled out as a word—opening into another and spiraling down, like the secret staircase behind bookshelves in old and haunted houses. I might, for instance, try the word "key." Only three letters, but also three parts of speech. There are noun-keys, cut by a locksmith, made for opening locks on doors (or books, or snails). There are also map keys, which are nouns, too, and sometimes referred to as a legend, a word that unfolds into its own treasure trove of meanings. But the key is made to help decode, another kind of opening. And haven't I read in a book somewhere that "key" is a different name for island, or a kind of island in tropical places where coconuts bob along the waves?

An adjective-key could be a "key decision," something essential, like me making this list to fold and stow in my Keyper. Verb-keys are all around us: the way my father "keys data" at work, punching numbers into a keyboard, which also has "key" in its name. And once my mother came home crying because someone had "keyed" her station wagon in the Safeway parking lot. Evidence of that "keying" (noun again!) is with us for many years, a light scar on the dark paint, as if a surgeon had made an incision…

Fourth draft

No surgeon, no incisions—just my friend laboring in the little round shack on the hill. No plumbing, no anesthesia—we're breathing together as she bears down. All the glass jars labeled and aligned on her handmade shelves. Wood floor mopped, counters scrubbed. Wavy glass paning the windows, barely holding back the night. Rug covered with a sheet. Her body seems all belly now, ready to burst. The midwife says *any time now, you can push.* Her husband hovers behind her, and she leans into him, though she has just discovered he's been having secret rendezvous in the city. But all that lies in wait: the dissolution of a marriage, solo life with baby, endless laundry runs into town, nights walking her son in a stroller across the bridge, over and over, until he falls asleep.

For now she still has to rely on him, and on me, the two of us propping her up, the two of us woefully inadequate to the task. We're only human, and this endeavor seems to require a power that is more than human. We've entered the realm of exhaustion that, paradoxically, feels amphetaminic, dawn appearing in the canopy just as the baby crowns. She screams, and he slithers out of her, trailing the umbilical cord.

I hold him just a few minutes later, his eyes open but still in the other world. He smells of blood and the sea. A thick warmth blurs his face, which, every second, becomes more human. *No*—a hollow echo—*stay unformed, not ours, for a just a little longer.*

When I try to write about this moment weeks later, I hear my pen scratch across the page as I cross out, and cross out. Language—even with all its nuance—does not seem up to this particular command. Each stroke's a nick, an abrasion, trying to scrape off the layers of the already known, but I can't get below the epidermal layer. I'm covered in scratches, small flesh wounds that will take forever to heal.

Fifth draft

The doctor says once, then repeats slowly: "Remember that healing is a process, not a deadline." I sit propped in an L-shape on the table, my broken leg freed from its cast only to be confined anew inside a knee-high walking boot.

"You know as a child, I wasn't allowed to have shoes with Velcro," I tell him, fingering the six places where I'll cinch the boot tight, secure it in place with the fuzzy fasteners. "It's ironic that something like this had to happen before I ever gave up my laces."

Dr. Knight is my junior by a couple of years and resembles one of those unobjectionably good-looking catalog men my mother hoped I would marry: clean-shaven, square jaw, broad shoulders that strain against his narrow white coat. His eyes widen when I speak, as if trying to discern why I tell him things that aren't germane to my medical history.

"Are you experiencing any pain?" he asks.

I shake my head. "Nothing physical. It *pains* me, though, that I can't run or spin or even trust myself to take the stairs on crutches."

"All in good time," he says, scribbling something in his notes, then closing the metal cover of his clipboard.

"I really like your notepad there," I gesture. "Good waterproofing. Do you have to be a doctor to get one of those?"

Dr. Knight cocks his head, regards me with a look I've seen before—the *are you for real? is that a serious question?* expression. "Honestly, I don't remember where this came from. It's just what I've always used." He shakes my hand and heads for the door.

Soon, a young nurse arrives, nodding shyly as she tucks thin sprigs of white-blond hair behind her ears. Her task is to show me how to wash my post-surgery wounds. "Be friends with the sterile gauzes," she says, and since English is not her first language, I lean in, listen more closely. "Gently, with peroxide, spraying both sides. See how the scar-shape is like interrupted smile. Go the whole way. Spray the whole smile."

I reach now for the steno book in my bag. Nadia thinks I'm taking notes on wound care, but that's only half true. I want to write about what has happened: the way sudden immobility alters our relationship to space, and more than space: to, our bodies, to our lovers' bodies, to our most basic kinds of mastery and our deepest, mortal fears. But how will I find the words to explain what I'm learning and then push further—to *conjure* that experience for someone who has never stood one moment and collapsed the next, skidding on slick tile over a ledge of concrete, the tibia and fibula severed the second they hit the ground?

Nadia touches my wrist with her cool, thin hand. "Funny, no? They call it *walking boot*, but you will not be walking."

I laugh and nod. Language *is* funny, is imprecise no matter how long you speak it, how long you study, no matter how much practice you have writing it down. "No weight to bear," she says, as she begins to wrap my foot with gauze. "But it is heavy, too, lugging the leg. We say no weight-bear, but we mean not pushing down. I'm sorry to say, it is a lot to carry after all."

Sixth draft

We are not the ones to carry my father's casket. Most of the weight, anyway, would not be *him*, not his body, which has already been lightened into dust by the coma in the end. The casket arrives before us, sitting on its casters above the open ground. Two navy officers stand at attention—stationed head and foot—throughout the service, backs straight, unmoving.

My brother's written a eulogy that makes everyone laugh. I sing a song, handing out copies of the music, hoping I'm on key, gesturing for the others to join me. They do, the words *May eternal light surround you* warbling toward the grave. But I'm more concerned about getting it right—the notes, the words, the intervals—so I'm not sure I'm even really singing to my father, or to what is left of him. A seven-gun salute happens somewhere in between the rabbi's sermon and the lowering of the coffin.

I help my mother shovel the first scoop of dirt, then we all follow suit, wet earth landing with thumps on the lid. A flock of crows whirls up in the far trees, cawing for attention. We want to take it as a sign of something, but their language remains inscrutable. One of my friends eschews the shovel and tosses in the earth with her bare hands. Some of us join in; the dirt sticking to our palms.

At some point I say to whoever is near me, *that was fun!*, and I don't know what I mean. I can't take it back, the word detonated in the graveyard. My friends are here, some colleagues I didn't expect; my brothers and their children. Even the receptionist from the nursing home has come to see my father off. My hands are dirty; I'm a little giddy.

For years after, I'll try to see this moment clearly. I'll recall snippets of black cloth, a single crow, wet earth in my palms. A white tent, rifle shots reverberating across the cemetery, the dog jumping out of my mother's arms. I'll want to revise it all—rewind, start another draft—but this version writes itself in stone.

Seventh draft

I always wanted to write something in wet cement—something that couldn't be revised—then perch on the curb or the playground fence, watching my bold inscription dry. But what would I write? Which combination of words should I choose to immortalize?

"Stop overthinking it!" all the kids jeered. "Just grab a stick and print *Julie was here.*"

We wrote our names in sand so often, sometimes encased in hearts or balloons, then waited for the tide to erase them. I liked that it was temporary, each day's blemished dune, how soon the smooth face of perpetual nothing reappeared along the shore.

"Parents leave their mark on you when they give you a name, but I want to leave a mark that's all my own."

"So have a baby!" April laughed. She was crimping her hair. She was cavalier. She might as well have suggested a milkshake or a trip to the mall. "You can put something really awesome on the birth certificate, like 'Baby Slurpee Jesus' or 'Seymour Butts.'"

Years in the future, contentedly childless, I write and deliver a eulogy for a different friend. Bob collaborates with me until the week before his death, when the cancer climbs his throat, renders him fully mute. "Read your poem, too," he made me promise—"the one with the *goddamn* in it. I want these Catholic fools to know I went to my grave an atheist."

He scribbled his epitaph on a legal pad: *I meant what I said.* Then, he remembered and threw up his hands: "They don't give you a stone if you're getting burned up, do they?"

Once, I wrote two sets of wedding vows, the first to the man I didn't marry, the second the woman I did. They float in memory now like long-tailed kites—one small diamond of misplaced devotion caught in a tree, fodder for nesting birds; another bright and box-shaped, aswirl with rainbows, stretching skyward above the raucous surf.

Once, I worked in an office with these words carved in the wall: *This sentence is not true.* I traced them with my finger every day for years, never venturing to contradict or concur.

Once, I saw a giant stone rising out of the waves in Maine. The engraving, preposterously large, proclaimed: *NOT ART.* How could I argue or agree?

Now on South Beach, an artist has commissioned a Poetry Rail, twelve poems permanently etched in metal using water jets. I am asked to contribute something. "Even when we're all under water," a new friend chirps, "your poem will be preserved forever!" No pressure, no pressure at all.

I reach back to everything I know about my life, griefs as inexpressible as joys, language necessary and futile at once, and then to those first words nested inside each other. I submit:

Grammar

Here, on the Atlantic, sunrise
the reversed syntax of my Seattle youth:

I marvel, still young, at what
it means to have been younger;

to see at last the *parent*
in *parenthesis*;

to read—for the first time—
whole chapters of my life

as an aside.

Final draft

Put them aside, for now: whole chapters you want to reread now that you know how the story ends. You used to do that all the time: close a book, hold it to your chest, then open to the title page, the table of contents, even the blank sheet that told you to pause a moment before embarking. You ran your hand across the type, knowledge crackling in your fingertips. A book read seems heavier than a book unread—as if your gaze, your attention, could be measured in ounces.

Once, for Father's Day, I sewed my father a tie. I didn't know how to sew. He didn't need a tie. I chose a silky navy blue that was difficult to work through the machine. I was twelve years old. My body had become something not ugly, exactly, but *ungainly*—all arm and leg and sharp pelvic bone. I folded and tacked and sewed uneven seams, wrapped the whole thing in tissue paper. I can't remember his face when he opened it, or if he even pretended to put it on. I remember only the sewing, each wrong stitch begetting another.

Before his last gurgled breath; before the hospice nurse said *there's no radial pulse*; before the shutting down and shutting off; before all his body heat compressed in his heart; before I cupped my hand and said *your family loves you*; before the inhale without an exhale—my mother and I watched him, hypnotized, the way one might watch a baby sleep. The room was too cold, and we huddled together under a blanket, not knowing we could ask for the heat to be turned up. We accepted what was offered us.

He died at 3:45 AM The night crackled around us as we waited for the mortician to arrive; we sat in the family room at hospice house, and I began to write his obituary. I tried to get beyond mere fact, to distill into the narrow column what can be known about a life. But I kept thinking about an early memory—one that won't be recorded—of flying a kite on the cul-de-sac of my childhood home.

I see my dad there, behind the video-cam, coaxing me to smile. I can see the heavy camera on his shoulder, one eye shut, lips parted as he concentrates on his sullen daughter. It's a cloudy day, and I'm wearing a coat that makes it difficult to move.

That girl, she wants to be light-hearted—for him. She wants to enjoy the tug of a kite as it grapples with the air. Her father says *start running, it will lift!* But she doesn't want this responsibility; to be a tether for something that insists on flying away. She freezes on the spot and refuses to meet her father's gaze, scowls while the string goes limp in her hand.

And it will be written like this forever: afraid of holding on, afraid of letting go.

Epilogue

The following piece is an excerpt from a month-long correspondence that sought to bear witness to our individual experiences of the COVID-19 pandemic.

The In-Between:
Letters from Isolation

May 16, 2020

Dear Julie,

On the news yesterday, pundits and late-night hosts kept repeating the words of a whistleblower scientist testifying before Congress: "2020 will be the darkest winter on record." There were many jokes with Game of Thrones references (*winter is coming...*), but every time I heard the phrase, I tried to parse its syntax: Did he mean the whole year of 2020 would be winter-like, in the sense of darkness and deprivation? Or did he mean that next winter, several months from now, would be doubly dark because of the concurrence of flu season with COVID-19? But the winter season slips into 2021. It doesn't really matter which he meant (in the end, it just means *things are BAD, people*), but I couldn't shake the sentence from my English-teacher mind loop.

This spring here has been particularly beautiful, maybe that's why. It's the time of year we look forward to for months, in particular because of the lengthening days, affording us easy-going evening walks after dinner, the sun setting in a slightly different place each night. It's difficult to coordinate *dark winter* with *lovely spring*. I get a delivery of farm fresh produce every other week, and just yesterday a local farmer (who used to be my student) left an order of two spring chickens at my door. And at the same time I felt terrible that I have so much when others have so little.

How do we reconcile the opposites in our lives? Joy with despair, abundance with scarcity, dark with light? How do we occupy that narrow space in the middle, with a modicum of grace?

Thinking of you,
Brenda

May 18, 2020

Dear Brenda,

How I wish I had answers to your questions! It's the see-saw of existence, isn't it, the way we're always wishing we could balance on the fulcrum without tipping too far either way. *Everything in moderation* our implicit wish, with the struggle always set against extremes.

I'm writing to you from our old apartment, which I don't think of as *old* yet really—it's the place we still sleep and eat, the place where we shower and dress and live with our kitties until Friday. Then, the movers come to transfer the heavy furniture—bed, couch, cat trees, dining table, et al.—from one residence to the other.

In truth, though, I'm writing from an interstice. We came "home" for lunch, and then the sky split open, launching the first of our summer storms. All the boxes and bags we were planning to take back with us to our other "home" are now piled up by the door, but it doesn't make sense to go out in this rain, the sky streaked purple and gold, lightning like graduation tassels.

Now that we're both quietly working, the cats have settled, too. They don't like watching their belongings—for everything we have is *theirs*—shuffled and dusted, folded and zipped away. Tina, our young cat, rushes to the high-pitched whine of packing tape being torn while Tybee, our elder cat, cannot bear it. The sound induces seizures, as does the crinkling of bags and wrapping paper.

I've always enjoyed summer storms, though I find them frightening when I'm driving to campus. I lean forward and clench the steering wheel so tight my nail marks are visible now. I suppose since I'm no longer commuting, I should appreciate the reprieve from car stress. Instead, I worry about other things: power failures, my own potential failures while teaching my class on Zoom.

Our building announced on Saturday that tomorrow (Tuesday) all power and water will be shut off for the whole day. An email was circulated; then signs posted in stairwells and on the elevator doors. Management's suggestion was that people make arrangements to leave home for the day and stay with family or friends, perhaps check into a hotel! I gaped as I read the caveats about staying in a dark, sweltering place all day with no internet or phone. No A/C. No front desk staff. No elevators or lights.

Surely some people sheltering at home are bed-ridden with the virus. Surely some people sheltering at home are sick with other things or fearful that what they have *is* the virus. Many people in our building are elderly, retired, facing chronic conditions, just trying to rest if not recover. Many others, like us, are working from home, whether for the short-term or the long. This isn't a simple matter of inconvenience, but a matter of safety, of unconscionable risk.

When I wrote to the building manager, he replied only that "These are challenging times for everyone. Please make accommodations accordingly."

At least one person in our building is scheduled to teach a four-hour poetry class on Zoom tomorrow afternoon. She will now be doing so while sitting on the bare floor of her new home office, computer tethered to her phone's data plan (with her partner's help, of course). She will be even more worried than usual about how the technology will hold, but also worried that her worry will show through and contaminate the warm dynamics of her class. She will still give breaks, encouraging her students, and herself, to stand up, stretch, drink some water, have a snack. She will be uncomfortable, most likely, and nervous, too. Still, she knows how lucky she is to have these as her most pressing complaints.

Go ahead—tell me what's vexing you, no matter how large or small. And tell me what you're wishing for, too, while you're at it. Pretend I'm a fountain at the mall.

With love, and evening rain,
Julie

May 22, 2020

Dear Julie,

What does it take to love this world completely?

That's the question that keeps whispering in my mind this morning. Where I'm sitting now—in my guest room/office, too cold to be on the porch—I have other people's words surrounding me. Like these, from Tina Schumann, a poet I know from teaching at the Rainier Writing Workshop:

> From the pea vines to the dandelions
> I am making it up as I go along.
>   Each step
>   —a worn declaration; *be here, love this...*

I want to *be here.* I want to *love this.* I even want to follow those ellipses with my breath. But so many un-nameable things are vexing me these days. They seem to alight in the branches of leafing-out trees or waver behind billowing clouds at sunset. I sometimes feel myself in a kaleidoscope, the colors swirling around me, beautiful but chaotic.

I'm not sure what will happen next, if *anything* will happen next, or if we'll be stuck in this place of in-between forever. Like your computer when it hits the wall and gives you the spinning pizza wheel while it tries and tries to get past whatever stalled it. Sometime you just have to re-boot, start all over again.

Sighing and stuttering this morning,
Brenda

May 26, 2020

Dear Brenda,

I can feel the struggle in your words, and I'm sorry it has taken me so long to read them!

The day you wrote was the day our movers came. My students submitted 46 poems, the length of a full collection, all of which I read and savored, though I labored over my words of response. *How to strike just the right balance between support and challenge, when to push and when to praise?* I have been teaching for eighteen years, and I still don't know the answer.

Angie's birthday was on Sunday, a day of prodigious rain accompanied by tornado warnings for our county. We couldn't even drive to see the burrowing owls she loves, as every road was flooded and muddy, the winds tossing garbage bins, flinging the mailboxes open like a row of gaping mouths.

Now I am sitting at my desk, a warm cat basking in the sun beside me, towering boxes of books all around. Moving out is different from settling in. Outside the tree that lavishes our lawn and car with star-shaped pink blossoms has two names—*frangipani* (higher-order name) and *plumeria* (lower-order name). Two such luscious names for a single living thing, yet so many experiences and emotions in this world seem to lack a name at all. If we were fluent in every language of the world, would we find a way to say all that pains and mystifies us? Or is a caesura deep as a canyon carved forever into the hard stone between feeling and saying?

Mary Oliver wrote of the "refined anguish of language," a phrase which has always stayed with me. I ran at the beach for the first time in two months today, and my heavy breath was its own kind of reverie, its own version of prayer. When I returned home, the news headline read, "U.S. experiences deadliest day of coronavirus as states begin to reopen." *Too soon? Too late? What's best or worst?* I am certain of nothing, not even the questions.

This weekend I learned there's a word for the space between the attic and the roof, or the top of a kitchen cabinet and where it meets the wall. *Soffit.* I've heard it before, but I had forgotten the context. Tina, our spry feline sleuth, leapt from the countertops into the slim empty space beneath the cupboards and the ceiling. She didn't want to come down, though we coaxed and coaxed.

She was being a soffit, bridging a gap. I want to be a soffit too, to place myself in the in-between and fill a longing, ease a grief. Maybe the mask I wear becomes a soffit, preventing an exchange of air with strangers? Maybe the blood I give becomes a soffit, too, as it enters the veins of strangers? Or maybe this is only wishful thinking. Still, I hope this letter might be a kind of soffit, too, closing the long distance between us, an envelope in your inbox that flickers as if to say *Open me! I've arrived.*

With love,
Julie

May 27, 2020

Dear Julie,

Today I write to you from a soffit: my attic loft, a long narrow space that is not really a room, not really an attic, but something in-between, a gap I fill with my chair from Ikea, an old futon that serves as a day bed, and myself. My dog—almost fourteen years old now—sometimes makes the trek upstairs with me, though the steps now scare her. She's figured out an odd, sideways kind of gait that gets her up with a minimum of slippage, and always when her little face appears at the top, she grins with triumph and lopes toward me, tongue out, ready for a treat.

Her bravery in the face of adversity is something to behold. Her faith that something good always waits at the end.

I began this correspondence with you toward the beginning of May from another in-between space, my front porch, and now here we are, almost at the end of this odd month, both of us moving from place to place, finding the landing pads where, for a little while, we can talk. Spring slips into summer, counties and states begin to re-open, and we still don't know what awaits us out there, in a world that is both so beautiful and so frightening at the same time. Rules keep changing, and we do our best to keep up.

On Monday, Memorial Day, my mom ached to go visit my dad at the cemetery. He was a vet of the Korean war, and this day always meant something to them. She wanted to go and pat his headstone, place a rock to mark our presence. But the Willows—her senior living community—is still on lockdown. They've started to ease restrictions a little bit; each floor now has a complicated walking schedule, and my mom can't seem to keep it straight. She always seems to be in the wrong place at the wrong time. Her skin is looking pale and drawn; she wears her mask low on her face, barely affording any protection at all. I print up her schedule in a way I hope will make more sense, but she flaps it helplessly in her hands.

She'll get past it, as I know we all will emerge from this hiatus, changed in ways we can't even imagine right now. We'll need to contemplate our obstacles, like my dog at the bottom of the staircase, and figure out new ways to move through this world. But for now, I sit and listen to the various tongues of birdsong, watch the sign language of trees, smell the semantics of earth after a hard rain. We are vessels of translation—always open, always arrived.

With love,
Brenda

Acknowledgments

We are grateful to the following journals that originally published these collaborative works:

Creative Nonfiction: "Toys"
Georgia Review: "Works-in-Progress"
Jet Fuel Review: "Dreams"
The Kenyon Review: "Camera"
Lunch Ticket: "Never"
The Normal School: "Bridges: A Catalog"
Punctuate: "Exercise"
Rappahannock Review: "Heat Index"
River Teeth: "Telephone"
Zone 3: "Mixed Drinks"

"Bridges: A Catalog" also appears in *The Spirit of Disruption: Landmark Essays from* The Normal School (Outpost19, 2018).

"Heat Index" also appears in *They Said: A Multi-Genre Anthology of Contemporary Collaborative Writing* (Black Lawrence Press, 2018).

BRENDA MILLER is the author of five essay collections, most recently *An Earlier Life* (Ovenbird Books, 2016). She also co-authored *Tell It Slant: Creating, Refining and Publishing Creative Nonfiction* and *The Pen and The Bell: Mindful Writing in a Busy World.* Her poetry chapbook *The Daughters of Elderly Women* received the 2020 Floating Bridge Press award. Her work has received six Pushcart Prizes. She is a professor of English at Western Washington University and associate faculty at the Rainier Writing Workshop.

JULIE MARIE WADE is the author of twelve collections of poetry and prose, including the poetry collection *Skirted* (The Word Works, 2021) and the memoir *Just an Ordinary Woman Breathing* (The Ohio State University Press, 2020). A recipient of the Lambda Literary Award for Lesbian Memoir and grants from the Kentucky Arts Council and the Barbara Deming Memorial Fund, Wade teaches in the creative writing program at Florida International University. She is married to Angie Griffin and lives in Dania Beach.

RECENT CLEVELAND STATE UNIVERSITY POETRY CENTER PUBLICATIONS

Edited by Caryl Pagel & Hilary Plum

POETRY

World'd Too Much: The Selected Poetry of Russell Atkins
ed. Kevin Prufer and Robert E. McDonough
Advantages of Being Evergreen by Oliver Baez Bendorf
Dream Boat by Shelley Feller
My Fault by Leora Fridman
Orient by Nicholas Gulig
Twice There Was A Country by Alen Hamza
Age of Glass by Anna Maria Hong
In One Form to Find Another by Jane Lewty
50 Water Dreams by Siwar Masannat
daughterrarium by Sheila McMullin
The Bees Make Money in the Lion by Lo Kwa Mei-en
Residuum by Martin Rock
Festival by Broc Rossell
Sun Cycle by Anne Lesley Selcer
Bottle the Bottles the Bottles the Bottles by Lee Upton

ESSAYS

I Liked You Better Before I Knew You So Well by James Allen Hall
A Bestiary by Lily Hoang

Codependence by Amy Long
The Leftovers by Shaelyn Smith

TRANSLATIONS

Scorpionic Sun by Mohammed Khaïr-Eddine, translated by Conor Bracken
I Burned at the Feast: Selected Poems of Arseny Tarkovsky translated by Philip Metres and Dimitri Psurtsev

For a complete list of titles visit www.csupoetrycenter.com